Praise for *Pow*

"I love this book! **Power Words** *is perhap.
book ever written on the influence that ou.
has on our lives. In an easily accessib.
demonstrates the energy and effe* — use.
Highly recommended, this book can change *your life."*

— **Denise Linn**, Author, *The Secret Language of Signs* and *Sacred Space*

"Your words carry energy, and they shape your life. In **Power Words** *Sharon Anne Klingler helps you to become a maestro of your words—appreciating them, loving them, choosing them in ways that steer your life toward your heart's desire. This book will forever change your relationship with words, the most intimate companions of your mind. I highly recommend it."*

— **Donna Eden**, Author, *Energy Medicine*

"Sharon Anne Klingler has written the book I wish I had! **Power Words** *takes all the elements of instant creation and puts them into doable, fun, empowering exercises we can all choose in the snap of a finger. A new, fresh take on the simplicity of creation itself."*

— **Dee Wallace**, Actress, Author, International Speaker, and Radio Host

"What a simple but brilliant idea! Sharon Anne Klingler brings a heightened awareness to this ever so important thing we do every day. She provides countless examples so that you can ignite your own life with the power of words. I love this book!"

— **Michele Takei, Ph.D.**, Author, *She-Q* and *Mandala Magic*

*"***Power Words** *helped me see the subtle ways I create my life every day. Sharon's exercises are effective, simple, inspiring, and they work very quickly!"*

— **Mary McCann**, Actress, Atlantic Theater Company Member

"As a practicing psychologist and hypnotherapist, I've incorporated the principles in **Power Words** *with my clients. I believe that therapists of every stripe will find* **Power Words** *applicable as a powerful intervention and homework tool. This book also lends itself to those in the world of interpersonal communication, advertising, and marketing. Most surprising, Sharon's book installed an unconscious positive technique in me that fits my psychology. I recommend this book to all who are on a path of personal growth. It's full of simple exercises, examples, and wisdoms that can help anyone and everyone!"*

— **Michael Freedman, Ph.D.**, Psychologist

POWER WORDS

ALSO BY SHARON ANNE KLINGLER

Books

Secrets of Success: The Science and Spirit of Real Prosperity
(with Sandra Anne Taylor)*

Intuition & Beyond

Life with Spirit

The Magic of Gemstones and Colors

Guided Visualizations and CD Programs

Drawing on Your Intuition
(kit with instruction book, CD, and colored pencils)

Divine Connections

Healing Journeys

Higher Realms, Higher Powers

Openings

Travel into Your Past Lives

*Available from Hay House

Please visit:

Hay House USA: www.hayhouse.com®
Hay House Australia: www.hayhouse.com.au
Hay House UK: www.hayhouse.co.uk
Hay House South Africa: www.hayhouse.co.za
Hay House India: www.hayhouse.co.in

POWER WORDS

Igniting Your Life with Lightning Force

Sharon Anne Klingler

HAY HOUSE, INC.
Carlsbad, California • New York City
London • Sydney • Johannesburg
Vancouver • Hong Kong • New Delhi

Published and distributed in the United States by: Hay House, Inc.: www
.hayhouse.com® • **Published and distributed in Australia by:** Hay House Australia Pty. Ltd.: www.hayhouse.com.au • **Published and distributed in the United
Kingdom by:** Hay House UK, Ltd.: www.hayhouse.co.uk • **Published and distributed in the Republic of South Africa by:** Hay House SA (Pty), Ltd.: www.hayhouse
.co.za • **Distributed in Canada by:** Raincoast Books: www.raincoast.com • **Published in India by:** Hay House Publishers India: www.hayhouse.co.in

Cover design: Julie Davison • *Interior design:* Nick C. Welch

All of the stories in this book are true. However, all names have been changed
to protect the privacy of the individuals involved.

The author of this book does not dispense medical advice or prescribe the use
of any technique as a form of treatment for physical, emotional, or medical problems without the advice of a physician, either directly or indirectly. The intent of
the author is only to offer information of a general nature to help you in your quest
for emotional and spiritual well-being. In the event you use any of the information
in this book for yourself, which is your constitutional right, the author and the
publisher assume no responsibility for your actions.

Library of Congress Cataloging-in-Publication Data

Klingler, Sharon A.
Power words : igniting your life with lightning force / Sharon Anne Klingler.
  pages cm
  ISBN 978-1-4019-4179-6 (pbk.)
1. Change (Psychology). 2. Language and emotions. I. Title.
BF637.C4K55 2013
650.101'4--dc23
                          2013028693

Tradepaper ISBN: 978-1-4019-4179-6

17 16 15 14   5 4 3 2
1st edition, December 2013
2nd edition, January 2014

Certified Chain of Custody
Promoting Sustainable Forestry
www.sfiprogram.org
SFI-01268

SFI label applies to the text stock

Printed in the United States of America

*I dedicate this book
to my dear friend, Dr. Wayne Knoll—
a gift to his students at Georgetown University,
a treasure to all his family and friends,
and—in every way—the best of men.*

CONTENTS

PART IV: Lifting Words for an Elevated Life

PART V: Words to the Wise

PREFACE

The discovery of words is one of life's greatest adventures. My quest to discover the enormous energy of words started many, many years ago when a good friend and health-care professional, Loren Schuh, gave me one word to say in order to prevent injury when lifting heavy cartons. I tried it, and my body immediately jumped to attention—just by saying a single word! And it wasn't an action word, like a verb; it was just a simple, single noun. (Later you'll be surprised by what this very effective word is.)

I wondered then, if a specific, simple noun can stimulate a precise and very active response, what kind of power can be lurking in the other words we speak? I was determined to find out. Of course, this quest wasn't entirely new for me. The origins and meanings of words have long been a curiosity and even a passion of mine. Words communicate, but when their energy is focused, words take on a new life. They can become weapons in an arsenal, beacons in the dark, and catalysts for indescribable power. It is this power, this *force* of words—apart from all else—that began to fascinate me and move me in a very literal way.

When you say to someone, "I give you my word," it's meant to convey a promise. It's an absolute, unwavering promise of some future action or some unimpeachable truth. As I studied and worked with the energy of words, I began to realize that I was "giving my word" with every word I spoke or thought. Just imagine the kind of power you have at hand when each word holds the promise of action and a proclamation of truth!

It was this promise of action and truth that led me to understand and work with the energy of words in two different ways: *Words that **trigger** action* and *Words that **lift** you to a higher truth.*

And these two are the uses of word energy that I'd like to share with you in this book.

Although many of the words in the following pages certainly are positive, this is not a book about positive thinking. There have been many books about that subject written over the years, indeed over the centuries, but this is not one of them. This book is about using the energy of precise words to lift your own energy and to stimulate immediate mental, emotional, and physical responses. Some of these words may be new to you, but many of them are words you have known all your life. It is the *energy* of words that will cause you to experience them differently than you ever have before.

After a lifetime of using words only for their meaning and not for their force, it may be challenging to work with words in this new way. But learning to link with the force beyond meaning simply requires focus and discipline, which are readily available when you decide that optimum power and success are worth a little effort!

So try some of the Trigger Words and Lifting Words in this book for yourself. The old days of blithely using words for mere communication will be behind you, and you'll find yourself wanting to tap the great force that hides inside every single word. Like me, you'll discover that Power Words will do far more than just help you lift heavy cartons. They'll help you lift every endeavor, relationship, feeling, job, and experience to undreamed of heights and unparalleled joy!

PART I

THE ENERGY OF WORDS

*"We create the world every day
when we utter words."*

— HOWARD RHEINGOLD

Chapter 1

The Nature
of Words

*"It is the word . . . which builds the
universe and commands its power."*

— G. H. Bonner

Words create undeniable power in the world. You've seen
for yourself how words can inflate, crush, encourage, disappoint, and excite through your own life and across the world
stage. In World War II, Hitler's words spurred the Nazis toward
heinous action, while Churchill's and Roosevelt's words rallied a
world against them.

Even beyond this, words do much more than merely influence
the people who hear or read them. They carry their own power
and are an integral part of your electromagnetic field. They put
out energy, and they attract the same type of energy to you. They
also attract the people and situations that resonate to their energy.
Because of this, words can become your most significant resource
in manifesting the success you seek and in living a powerful and
incandescent life.

Throughout this book, we'll be working with words that you
can use for a multitude of reasons—making business decisions,
weight loss, help with creative projects, muscle strength, communication, healing, financial investments, relationships, breaking

addictions, tasks at work, and much more. In all of these, you'll be able to apply the energy of specific words for each task.

I call these words Power Words. And although they are not a new language, they are words that can be used in a new and different way. But in order to use a word's energy, you need to *know* the word's energy as well as its focus, feeling, and meanings at a deeper, inner level. For this you must really take the time to do the processes in this book—even if it's just for a minute or two. Once you open yourself to the power of words, you will be able to use them to trigger big results in every part of your life.

The Genesis Word

> *"In the beginning was the Word . . ."*
>
> — JOHN 1:1

The above quote is just one of many from the Bible that indicate the creative power of a word. It's not surprising that creation stories from around the world also begin with a word. Imagine what it would be like to see each word as a potential new beginning—the genesis of your future. Energetically it is!

Born from Word Power

Close your eyes and imagine that your entire future is bourne on the energy of your next word. It is the genesis—the birth and beginning—of what is to come for you. What word would you choose?

Choose it now, and take a moment to fill yourself with that word. Feel it, and see your whole life infused with its energy. Picture the actions that are born from this word, and sense the future it brings.

You can also use this process every morning to discover the genesis of your day. And you can use it any time to see what new beginning lies in that very moment. Whatever word you sense as your genesis, let it become a focus word for you. Really feel its energy; use it throughout your day, and see what it triggers for you. With your genesis words, you can take the steps to give rise to a whole new creation story of your own!

Word Energy You Can See and Feel

In his book *The Hidden Messages in Water,* Japanese scientist Dr. Masaru Emoto demonstrated the enormous power of words through photographs of water crystals under various conditions, including words that were shown and spoken to the water. Positive words (such as *wisdom, angel, thank you*) as well as kind sentiments (*You're cute* and *You're beautiful*) all formed more complete, beautiful, and symmetrical, crystals. But negative words and sentiments—such as *Satan, You fool!, You make me sick,* and *I will kill you*—created very incomplete, deformed, and quite ugly crystals.

Which do you think had the best influence of any of the words tested? "I have found the most beautiful crystal of all," said Emoto. "The one created by *love* and *gratitude.*"

Here's a brief process that lets you experience for yourself a little of what Emoto's water crystals experienced. The following are two very common, yet highly charged, emotional words that allow you to sense their energy easily.

Word Power Comparison

Close your eyes. For a few moments, simply think of the word *hate.* Really hold the idea in your mind and heart. Breathe the energy of the word *hate* into your body. Begin to notice how you feel emotionally and physically with the word *hate* filling your energy.

After a few moments take a deep breath and exhale—letting go of that word and its energy completely. Now replace it with the word *love*. As your breath gently comes and goes, fill every part of yourself with the energy of the word *love*. Feel the quality of *love* throughout every part of you. Notice how you feel in body, mind, and heart. After several moments of purposefully filling yourself with the word *love, notice the love you feel*—even for little things. Open your eyes, still filled with this serene and happy energy.

In this process, it was probably easy for you to sense the energy of these very different and emotionally charged words. The word *hate* may have made you recall people you dislike or people who have hurt you. You probably wanted to shake off that uncomfortable energy of *hate*. Some people even get agitated with the word, while others actually become hot. This isn't surprising since *hate* and *heat* have related base words in Old English. Many descriptions of anger include *heat,* such as *heated confrontation, hot under the collar, heat of battle, hot and bothered,* and so on.

With such energy, it's surprising how often the word *hate* is used. *I hate that shirt. I hate that restaurant. I hate that music.* Or even, *I hate those people.* While there may be many things, people, and moments in life that seem to fall short, is *hate* really the best word to express it? And even if it seems to be, do you really want the energy of hate in your life? A softer word might work better to shift that energy. Better still, rather than focusing on what you don't like, you can find a way to bring the word *love* and its energy to mind and heart during those disappointing moments.

I have a client, Marianne, who was very unhappy with her life. As we talked, I noticed how very often she used the word *hate*. I recommended that every time she used the word *hate* describing someone or something to change that word to *love*. At first, she *hated* the process! She said it felt like lying. I asked her to keep going nonetheless. It took a number of weeks to wear away the old pattern, but in the end it was all worth it. Her hatred turned—if not at first to love—to acceptance, tolerance, and nonresistance.

As an extension of the *love* she declared for others, she sought to understand those people. And she found that the things she had always hated simply weren't important enough to evoke that kind of energy. Even some of the food she had hated moved to her *like* list. Most important, Marianne started loving her life and herself more.

If *love* is the word that produced the most beauty and harmony that Dr. Emoto found, just think of what can happen when you express this word to yourself. Infusing the word *love* and its energy frequently into your daily experience helps you to love your life each day. I use it in my meditation practice and often throughout my day employing a powerful process with water, which you'll find in Part II. In the meantime, take a moment to repeat the word *love* and hold it in your heart several times during the day. You'll be surprised by how it will lift the level of love in your life—and in the world.

The Creative Force of Language

"For as the rain . . . waters the earth and makes it bring forth and sprout . . . so shall my word be. . . . It shall do what I please, and it shall accomplish that for which I sent it."

— Isaiah 55:10–11

In the same way that the rain brings forth the buds of the earth, the language you use brings forth the life that you create. And the words that you use over and over are the language that teaches you—and teaches the world about you. Your words are reflections—images of yourself. As you will see later, each and every word carries an image, an energy, and several qualities that you can put to powerful use.

Your language is the electrical current that moves through your life. And that current can be negative or positive. Even words that aren't as apparently negative as the word *hate* can carry a heavy energy, such as the word *swamped,* which many people use simply to indicate that they're busy.

On the other hand, there are other words that don't seem to have a beneficial emotional charge either, but are actually very positive—and can be made even more so. Take the word *intention.* It doesn't seem to carry too much of a punch, but you can really make it a positive reason for being. I use it as a Power Word, allowing it to bring a more extreme and focused energy to my purposes and intentions. Let's take a look at the words *swamped* and *intention* to see the creative forces they carry.

Out of the Swamp

Think about how you feel when you're so busy with mundane tasks and your other obligations that you don't have the time to do you it all—much less pursue your own important purposes.

Imagine that you're this busy now, and say the words *I'm swamped!* Close your eyes and take a deep breath, pulling those words inside you. Take a minute to really imagine yourself in a *swamp.* Put yourself there completely. How does it feel? Do you feel stuck? Are you struggling against the mud? Do you want to continue to create a swamped experience in your energy and your work?

Now take a cleansing breath, and with your exhalation let that all go. Then with another deep breath say to yourself the word *intention.* Bring in and feel the energy and strength of this word. Now say *intense intention.* You're not only struck by a great sense of your purpose, but you're also filled with the *intense* passion you feel for that purpose. Hold *intense intention* deep inside you, and feel the desire to bring your utmost attention to this dream. Every time you use *intense intention,* you notice that you're eager and excited to take action on your intention no matter how busy you are.

As you can see, *swamped* is something you may really not want to be. You also might want to think twice about using the words: *drowning in work, over your head,* or *bogged down*—which really only takes you from a swamp to a bog! Instead, let the word *intention* spur you onto greater power, focus, and force in pursuing your dream. Sometimes I even combine the words *intense* with *intention* and use the word *intension* to add a punch of energy! Give it a try.

More and more people are beginning to understand the great power of their thoughts. They seek their inner power through inspiring books, affirmations, and even daily meditation, an activity that I see as a real game changer. Yet, even with all that, if people don't change the words they use in their waking thoughts, their good work will be overrun by the negative current of their difficult histories and word patterns. For those who seek change, their everyday language must resonate with a new purpose—not just at special times of affirmations, but all the time. And Power Words can help you do that.

You create the language that creates your life. And what an opportunity that is! You can use your words not just to express your reality, but also to mold it—every hour, every minute, every thought, every utterance!

Two Different Types of Power Words

> *"All thought is creative! However, not all thought is constructive or positive."*
>
> — NAPOLEON HILL

Everyday words create your daily reality—both for good and bad. In this sense, *every* word you use is a power word because each carries its own creative power. What each word can create depends entirely on the word, its meaning, its energy, and how you use it.

Happily, there is a multitude of potent and positive success-producing Power Words—words that evoke a force that you can regularly use to aid with specific tasks, attract opportunity, and manifest success. And with just a little effort in their discovery and focus, you can put them to work for you. There are two types of Power Words:

1.   Trigger Words
2.   Lifting Words

1. Trigger Words are precisely chosen to be applied to specific situations in order to create success in those situations. Trigger Words can be single words or phrases that range from the simple and everyday to the extraordinary and unique. But regardless of how common or uncommon the word or phrase is, each is exactly chosen for a precise circumstance or activity. Throughout this book, you will find Trigger Words that can help you with very specific situations in business, home, relationships, health, creative projects, and even in breaking negative habits. From better posture to ending addictions, from choosing a stock investment to writing a book, these Power Words can help trigger your success.

Pulling the Trigger

Close your eyes and say the word *trigger*. Don't think about it; just fill yourself with its energy. Notice that as you repeat the word *trigger* you feel like something's just about to happen. You're filled with excitement. The word *trigger* triggers your response. And you know that every *Trigger* Word you use can put you in a state of readiness and propel you forward like a shot!

Trigger Words are not magic, but they do have a compelling force to them. Each word expresses distinctive energy, elicits specific responses, and causes certain effects. *Then, when you add your focus to the word's natural energy, you can direct that energy for precise and very successful results.* In just a few moments you'll experience firsthand the energy of one of these precise Trigger Words. In Part II, you'll find many more Trigger Words and learn how they can stimulate the results you seek. But, first, let's take a quick look at the second type of Power Words.

2. Lifting Words help elevate your levels of energy, creativity, opportunity, and joy. You never stop thinking words. They are your life-force energy. And in any given moment, you have the option of using words that lift or limit. Unfortunately, limiting language is the vocabulary we often use—sometimes unconsciously—to lessen, diminish, dismiss, or reject ourselves and others. Any words of judgment and intolerance are, by their very nature, limiting because they measure one's faults and shortcomings. When you engage in limiting language, you lessen your own energy, close the doors to opportunity, and shut down your own expansion—even if the judgment is of someone else.

You may ask why would your judgments and criticism about someone else—or even about a place or an event—lessen your life. It's because, regardless of their target, these types of words carry abrasive and limiting force, both in their meaning and in their energy. And since you are the one using them, you'll be the one feeling them.

Lifting Words, on the other hand, carry beneficial, strong, positive, and sometimes even bold meanings. Lifting Words can be very common, like *happy*—or even the word *lift*. But others are less frequently used words, such as *sublime, lofty,* and *exalted.* It's fun to find less common words to lift your energy, but everyday words are just as effective. For instance, how would your energy feel tonight if you were to insert the word *joy* into your language a hundred times today?

Lifting You Up

Close your eyes and say to yourself the word *lift.* Breathe deeply and repeat *lift* gently a few more times. Notice that you can feel your energy lifting up. You almost feel as if you're about to rise up—a little like a helium balloon ready to take off on a breeze. Every time you use a *Lifting* Word, you will feel lighter, your energy will be higher, and your perspective will soar to the sky!

All Lifting Words are best used by inserting them into your everyday thoughts and conversations. When you fill your language with them, they lift your energy, your outlook, your actions, and consequently, your life, in immeasurable ways. We'll discuss more about Lifting Words in Part IV. For now, let's look at Power Words that can trigger your immediate results.

Startling Results from Unexpected Words

You can put surprising word power in your hands! With Lifting Words, you can fill your entire language with power—not just anytime and anywhere, but all the time and everywhere. With Trigger Words, however, you actually direct a current of energy to specific situations and tasks at the very moment it's needed. It's like adding a surge of power right on target. Take a moment to do the following simple process completely before reading any further. *Really do it fully.* It may seem a little silly to you at first, but you'll soon understand why it's important.

Part I: No Word—No Power

Imagine, for a moment, that you've dropped something on the floor. Or, better yet, if you can, please actually drop a pen or a piece of paper, or anything, on the floor next to you.

If you are in a place where you can do so, stand up, bend over, and then pick up the virtual or real object. If you can't stand up, bend in your seat to pick it up. This will only take a moment—so, please, take the time to do this action now.

You probably noticed that you successfully picked up the object, but there wasn't much other beneficial energy to the task. You'll soon see that when you add a Trigger Word to the task, even to a simple task like this, everything changes.

Predetermined Trigger Words and phrases can help you take a specific action, do a particular job, change a singular pattern, create a new habit, or redirect certain energy. Some Trigger Words may be different from Lifting Words; some may be the same. It's the *way* you use them and the *reason* you use them that make the difference between the two. You would be surprised by the enormous variety of Trigger Words there are—and the diverse types of purposes they champion. You'll notice a big difference in your life between using Trigger Words and not using them. And you'll see just how much in a moment when you do Part II of the above process.

You can enlist the power of any specific word to impact mental focus, emotional response, activity level, and even physical and muscular reactions. With words you can shift the energy of any experience, great or small. **When you use a word, you invoke that energy. And you can apply that energy immediately.**

Part II: New Word—New Power

Take a moment to drop your pen or other item on the floor again. If you can, stand up and prepare to pick it up. You can also do this from a seated position if you must. This time, as you begin to bend over, say to yourself the word *abdominals*. Hold *abdominals* in your mind as you bend.

Notice that, as soon as you think *abdominals*, your focus goes immediately to your stomach area, and your abdominal muscles contract, supporting you fully. Repeat the word *abdominals* while you pick up your pen. Be aware of your posture as you do.

It's very easy to see the difference a Trigger Word can make—even one as purely technical as the word *abdominals*. It's also easy to realize how immediately responsive you are to such a word. I use this Power Word frequently. It was taught to me by a dear friend and health-care professional, Loren Schuh. And it has saved my back countless times.

I shared this Trigger Word with one of my students, Martha. She was an older lady who had hurt her back a couple of times when picking up different objects. She had become so concerned about having another injury that she even stopped picking up her cat. Once she began to add this simple, but very effective, Trigger Word, she became fearless. Martha used it every time she picked something up, and she hasn't had another injury since. She even got another cat!

You can use the Trigger Word *abdominals* whenever you pick up any object. Your muscles will be tighter, and you'll be more focused on the task. It will be an inner command to naturally use the correct posture for lifting.

Some Trigger Words command, some remind, some provoke, some motivate. Some catalyze, some excite, some focus, some calm. It's amazing how a simple word can actually alter the way you respond to a situation and—consequently—alter the outcome of that situation as well. And in time you'll find that you can trigger outstanding results just about anytime and anywhere.

Chapter 2

Deeper Meanings, Deeper Powers

"We learn that words have an independent life of their own, grown out of echoes and connotations and associations."

— James J. Kilpatrick

Every word carries an energy that can be sensed, regardless of whether you're thinking it, speaking it, hearing it, or reading it on the page. A lot of elements impact a word's energy, and the first is the word's meaning—or actually, meaning*s*.

Most words have several meanings and even more connotations. A lot of words have morphed into new words—just as *metamorphose* morphed into *morph!* There are also many words that now carry a whole different meaning than their original usage. For instance, one of the words that is often used when talking about high performance cars is *horsepower.*

Driving Word Power

Close your eyes, and think of the word *horsepower.* Bring the word *horsepower* into your mind and body. Begin to notice what you sense in your own energy and in your imagination.

Repeat the word *horsepower.* Take a deep breath, and notice everything you feel with *horsepower.* Even if it's subtle, what do you experience?

In this little word exercise, different people have different and multiple experiences. When I do this exercise, I am often driven— pun intended—to move or take action. Some people imagine the vibration of a running motor. Some recall an auto commercial or the excitement of getting a new car. Others may feel like they're in the driver's seat of a sports car. Or they imagine the *vroom* of a motor. Some people are fueled with energy, and many may experience a combination of these.

Of course, some people might have gotten an image of galloping horses. One of my students in a Word Energy class was actually moved to recall the horseback riding she had done as a teenager. But of all the many responses, it's unlikely that anyone would have had the image of a horse raising a 550-pound weight the distance of one foot in one second, which is the original definition of the word. Clearly the original meanings of many words don't stretch far enough to cover what they mean now and how they feel to everybody.

This little thought experiment also shows how word energy can be perceived. *From the actual meaning and its meaning to you; to having conceptual, visual, and audial perceptions; to feeling emotions, sensing vibration, triggering memories, and more—every word has its own energy and tells its own story.*

Words Never Come Up Short

Perhaps you wouldn't think that small technical words with precise meanings would give as many feelings, images, and diverse perceptions as a word like *horsepower.* But they actually do. Let's take a look at a pair of opposite words that are simple descriptions of size, yet they still illustrate how vast the experience of word energy can be.

Itty-Bitty Word Power

Close your eyes, take a deep breath, and relax. Begin to hold the word *short* in your mind and in your heart. Repeat the word *short*. Fill yourself with *short* in every way. Notice how it almost makes you feel smaller—in your body and your energy.

Now take another deep breath, and let go of that word and all of its energy as you exhale. Release it completely and replace it now with the word *tall*. Say the word *tall* to yourself each time your breath comes and goes, and feel the energy of *tall*. Sense what happens and every response and image. Notice everything you feel emotionally, mentally, and physically when you're filled with the energy of *tall*.

If you're like most people, during this process, you probably felt—at least at a subtle level—a diminishment or shrinking of your energy with the word *short*. You may have even begun to slouch a little or imagined yourself smaller. Conversely, with the word *tall*, your energy probably grew, making you feel larger or even causing you to sit up straighter. The words *short* and *tall*—as simple as they may be—affected your experience.

This little process illustrates how words influence your energy. Those that limit—even spatially—can diminish your experience, while literal lifting words actually do elevate. It shows that every word carries a deeper meaning and force. And it illustrates how you have to bring words deep inside you in order to discover the energy, images, and influence they carry. (We'll see more about the word *tall* in Chapter 7.)

Stop Thinking

For many the imagination is a tool of pretending only. But don't let yourself get fixed on this idea. Indeed, try not to get fixed on any idea at all. **There is nothing so potentially perilous as a fixed belief.**

Webster's Dictionary tells us that an image is "a mental picture of something; a conception; idea; impression." It is a mental process that comes through the right brain, or the imaging side of the brain. Many people are hesitant to use—and trust—their imaginations. They feel that the images and perceptions they experience have an unreal quality because they're "only imagining" them. But in truth, they are actually *imaging* those perceptions through the right brain.

> *"I never came upon any of my discoveries through*
> *the process of rational thinking."*
>
> — ALBERT EINSTEIN

Even for scientists, accountants, and those whose work depends on analysis and rational thinking, the process of discovery and creativity happens in more imaginative ways. The left parietal lobe, or left brain, performs math and measurement functions and helps with deductive reasoning and statistical conclusions. It will help you balance your checkbook and convert quantities from ounces to cups and dollars to Euros. But your imagination is the key to your creativity and discovery.

What Do You Think?

Close your eyes and take a moment to command yourself, *Think, think, think.* You may feel like you're being disciplined, almost like you're supposed to remember or analyze something. Feel the force of *thinking.*

Now let that go and give yourself the command, *Imagine, imagine, imagine.* It immediately moves you from heaviness to lightness. Say the word *imagine* again. It seems to carry an air of expectancy and a freedom that lifts you. With it you become eager to find and create everything *imaginable.*

Only your imagination allows you to fully experience the books that you read. Even though books are made up of words, your experience of them is filled with images and concepts. When you see a film of a book that you've already read, the film images will be very different, because you're seeing the director's imagining of the book, not yours.

Reading not only relies on your imagination, it also helps *build* your imagination. The more you develop your imaging muscle through reading, the greater ease you will have in visualizing and in trusting all of your perceptions. So keep reading, keep imaging, keep imagining, and keep discovering.

Never invalidate any experience because it "only" feels like your imagination. It's your most important mental resource, and it's trying to tell you something. When you embrace the broader vision of your imagination, you find a deeper meaning in life that invites loftier ideas. As Einstein said, "Imagination is more important than knowledge."

It helps you discover loftier words, too. In working with words—imaging is also an immeasurable tool. You can use your imaging to experience a word's deeper meaning and energy. You'll also use it in working with Trigger Words. When Einstein used his imagination, he called it a thought experiment—a tool he used successfully throughout his life.

Thought Experiments from Einstein to You

Thought experiments are performed by anyone who uses the mind along with its imaging and conceptual faculties in order to create new ideas, draw conclusions, or solve problems. There are no petri dishes or microscopes in a thought experiment, except those that might be in your mind. For instance, Edison's thousands of tests looking for a filament for the lightbulb were actual experiments, but theoretical physicists must rely on thought experiments to draw conclusions about M-theory, string theory, and so on.

Of course, theoretical physicists aren't the only scientists who have used thought experiments to create breakthrough science. Almost every actual experiment ever done was preceded by an idea—a concept—in the scientist's mind.

Accountants and businessmen often have a challenge with imaging and trusting their imaginations. I had one client who wanted to learn to work with words, but he, too, had trouble imaging. I gave my client, an accountant named Rob, the assignment to choose any word throughout his day that comes up in conversation, like *book, cake,* or *pen.* I asked him to take 30 seconds in that moment to use his imagination to see, feel, sense, or even taste and smell the imaginary *book, cake,* or *pen.* I asked him to do this with various words five to ten times a day for two weeks. Within one week, Rob had become much more comfortable with his imaging process and thought experiments.

Einstein seemed to live in a continuing process of thought experiments, one of which he revisited for years. He would imagine himself riding on a beam of light, looking in a mirror to discover what he would see. His conclusions from this imagery eventually changed what the world knows about time and space.

Spatial, conceptual, and imagery functions occur in the right hemisphere of the brain, the imaging center of the mind. Even if you don't realize it, your mental meanderings are a sort of thought experiment, too. From Copernicus to Newton, from Einstein to you—thought experiments create the reality you know.

Just Imagine!

Everybody perceives things differently. Some people who are very left-brained and analytical by nature may have a little difficulty in allowing spontaneous perceptions to occur. Some people are more audial, yet others tend to be more visual.

However you perceive, you can expand your influence—and shift your personal energy—through Power Words. In fact, this undeniable force of words is already cascading through your energy and ceaselessly impacting your life. Even words that you've heard a million times have energies you might never realize—until you go within to tap their power.

"For all who but strive,
who will but use untried forces, unknown energies,
there are un-gathered riches, . . .
un-won crowns yea, an unrevealed heaven."

— M ARY E. B AIN

You may never have used the types of methods you'll find in this book before. They could be your "untried forces." But try them, and keep trying. A Power Word is just a word unless you tap the force of it by breathing deeply and focusing on the word's interior energy. So bring each word inside you—in your mind, your heart, and your body. Hold it. Feel its energy, and use it. Be sure to close your eyes intermittently as you read the text of each process. This will help you shut out external distractions and go deep within the word to feel its power.

These processes can help you discover the "unknown energies" of words and help you capture the "ungathered riches" they can bring. So get ready to put your right brain to work. Each and every time you use a Power Word, give your imagination the job. It will be a thought experiment that will direct the power of your life. And soon, like Einstein, you may find yourself riding on a beam of light that illuminates and transforms your world!

Chapter 3

Discovering the Energy of Words

*"We see words that blow like leaves in the winds of autumn
—golden words, bronze words, words that catch
the light like opals."*

— JAMES J. KILPATRICK

There are many, many layers of a word's energy, and each impacts your experience and your own energy differently. The elements of word energy are:

- Meaning
- Imaging and sensing
- Emotional energy
- Vibration and frequency
- Color
- Shape and form

Let's take a look at these divergent forces of words and discover how you sense them—and how they impact your own energy.

Meaning

The meaning of a word is a powerful thing. It does much more than define the word; it actually packs a punch of energy. Of course, it's easy to see how much power comes with words such as *hate, sex, love,* and others that naturally have an emotional component. But, as we've also seen, simple words have great power, too. Even words that have very precise technical meanings express distinctive qualities in energy.

Word Power That Measures Up

Close your eyes and take a relaxing breath. Think of the word *inch,* and bring it inside you. Notice what happens in your energy. Say *inch* to yourself again. What do you perceive? Take some time to feel it completely.

After a moment, take a deep breath, and release the word *inch* as you exhale. Now think of the word *mile.* Really fill your entire experience with the word *mile.* Immediately notice what happens in your imaging, sensing, and energy.

Although these are even more precisely defined, you probably felt a shrinking and then enlarging energy, as you had with *short* and *tall.* But unlike *short* and *tall,* your perceptions here probably felt more lateral than vertical. You may have perceived a narrowing energy with the word *inch,* or you felt your attention focus on an imaginary inch-sized space in front of you. Then, with the word *mile,* your energy widened, and so did your attention with it. You may have even felt that you wanted to stretch your arms out wide or that your body was—in your imagination—expanding horizontally.

This is a clear example of how meaning carries energy. Even though these two words seem to have no emotional value at all, you were immediately able to feel the difference between them. Indeed, *mile* has such a *broad* emotional impact. I have a client, Sam, who uses *mile* when he wants to feel "larger" in his confidence—before meetings and presentations at the international company where he works—or whenever he wants his influence and energy to be a *mile* wide! As you will see in Part II, you can even use *inch* and *mile* word power to measure your choices when a decision has to be made.

Imaging and Sensing

> *"Uttering a word is like striking a note on the keyboard of the imagination."*
>
> — LUDWIG WITTGENSTEIN

Every word carries an image, and that image coincides, in part, with the word's meaning. Beyond that, your personal history and the workings of your own imagination will determine what you perceive visually with any given word.

Sensing the energy of words can occur physically or conceptually. With sensing you may imagine a sound or think of a part of your body. You may actually sense a tactile feeling, or perceive subtle nuances in your own energy. When this occurs, allow yourself to fully experience it and trust what's happening for you. When you give yourself over to everything that happens, you find that even sensing physical energy isn't hard. Well, unless *hard* is the word you want to experience!

Hard Word Power

Close your eyes, and take a deep breath. Hold the word *hard* in your mind. As you repeat *hard* slowly several times, notice what you sense in your imaging, your body, and your energy. Feel everything as you bring *hard* fully into you.

After a moment, let the word *hard* go, and with another breath, pull the word *soft* inside you. Fill yourself with *soft*, as you say the word to yourself a few more times. Become the energy of *soft*, and observe everything you image, sense, and experience.

If you really allowed yourself to experience the subtle energies during this process, you could feel the difference in the power of *hard* and *soft*. You may have even noticed your body tensing a bit with the word *hard* and relaxing with the word *soft*. How much more might you sense with words that carry even more emotional meaning and energy?

Emotional Energy

> *"Things must be felt with the heart."*
>
> — HELEN KELLER

The emotional power of words is evident in each person's life. Think back and ask yourself how many of the unkind words that were spoken to you do you remember? How many of the compliments? Emotionally charged words have the power to wound or heal, to reject or embrace, to hurt or make happy. Even when you're not the focus of emotional words, you can still feel their energy.

Word Power with Feeling

Close your eyes and begin to relax. Now, let yourself pull the word *hurt* into your heart. Hold it there and repeat *hurt* for several moments. Notice how you sense the word *hurt* in your energy and your experience. Notice everything you feel.

Take a deep breath and let go of the word *hurt* with your exhalation. With your next breath, pull the word *happy* into your heart completely. Feel the power of *happy* inside you, as you repeat this word. Notice the images, energy, and feelings you sense with the word *happy.*

As you can see, holding a word in your heart gives you a very vital experience of its emotional energy, one that you can feel in your entire being. You may have experienced some discomfort and a sense of heaviness or darkness with the word *hurt,* while you certainly may have had a perception of a joyful lightness or bright colors with the word *happy.*

The emotional energy of many words can be universal, feeling much the same for most people because of their meanings. But there is a deeper emotional value that can vary significantly based on each individual's personal history. For people with a lifetime of *hurt,* their experience of that word will be more severe than those with a happier past. And even for those with a *happy* history, the word *hurt* may bring up specific memories of painful moments or hurtful people in their lives.

I had a client named Helen who was a very young girl in a concentration camp during World War II. She had lost most of her family. But thanks to her only surviving uncle, she made her way to the States. Many years passed before she came to me, but even though it had been a very long time, her pain had not healed. When she worked with the word *hurt,* her memories of that pain sprang back to life. For her, the word *hurt* equaled *Nazi* and was synonymous with horror, death, intolerance, and a host of extremely negatively charged emotions. Helen worked diligently for many years on healing her history and changing her present focus. Eventually the word *hurt* only referred to the arthritis in her fingers and was almost permanently replaced by the word *happy.* As for the world as a whole, it may take several more generations to come and go before the negative energy of the word *Nazi* is dissipated.

The emotional power of words may be the most important and impactful of all the different energies they carry. This is why it's *so* important to choose words carefully. Later in the book we'll be taking a deeper look at emotionally charged words. But if you're ever curious about the emotional power that any word carries, all you have to do is hold that word in your heart. You'll be able to feel it completely.

Vibration and Frequency

"Words have weight, sound, and appearance."

— WILLIAM SOMERSET MAUGHAM

In physics the term *frequency* refers to wave vibration. Every sound and every word that is spoken or sung emits a wave that carries its own frequency. For most people the frequency of sounds—whether from the spoken word, music, or noise—affects other senses, including the imaging center of the brain. This experience of cross-sense association is called *synethesia*. Though most people have it to some degree, there are some who experience it significantly.

In *The Glass Menagerie* the "little silver slipper of a moon" is seen "rising over Garfinkel's Delicatessen." With these two very divergent phrases, Tennessee Williams uses not only meaning, but also sound and shape to juxtapose soft fantasy with hard reality, a theme he successfully portrays throughout this classic of American theater. No doubt, when you read these two descriptions, you could *feel* the difference yourself.

This ability of the brain to combine information helps us understand how frequency can evoke feeling and idea. For instance, words and sounds with high tones cause a sense of lightness and smallness, while low-pitched sounds and words can feel heavy and large.

Still, even more than the wave frequency of sound, each word—even when it's not spoken—carries a vibration that can impact your other senses. This vibration can cause you to sense heavy or light, cold or hot, bright colors or dark.

Sensory Word Power

Close your eyes and take a deep breath. With your inhalation, pull the word *hot* inside you. Hold the word *hot* in your mind, in your heart, and in your body. Repeat *hot* several times for at least a minute or two. Notice how you feel, and notice the energy, images, and colors that you experience, as *hot* fills you completely.

After a few minutes, take another deep breath and with the exhalation send the energy of *hot* away. Then with your next breath, bring in the word *cold.* Fill yourself with *cold,* and notice what immediately happens. Repeat the word *cold* softly and slowly, as *cold* energy fills your body. Notice any perceptions in energy, images, or colors that come to mind.

Clearly, there is a vibration and resonance in every word. Indeed, if you had held the word *hot* in your inner focus for several more minutes, you might have actually become warm or, perhaps, jittery or tingly with nervousness. When I hold the word *cold* too long, I actually start to shiver as you would in cold weather. Such is the nature of vibration and frequency. Frequency gives you a chance to *feel* words—and see them in a new light and a new color.

Color

The condition of cross-sense association extends into color, as well. In his February 2012 article on synesthesia in *The Economist,* Mike Gerra shares "that spoken sounds and the symbols which represent them give rise to specific colours." The color associations with words are influenced by meaning, emotional energy, frequency, and vibration.

For instance, your experience of the word *hot* may have elicited the colors red, orange, and/or yellow. That's a very natural response for most people. The word *cold* very likely stimulated darker colors, such as blue or black. But even if you perceived other colors with these words, you're still synesthetic. Your experience is unique to yourself. All of the thought experiments in this chapter allow you to discover how *you* sense the energy of words. You may not think you're synesthetic, but you can sense the colors of words when you "look" for them. Let's take a look now at the colors of two very different emotional words.

Colorful Word Power

Take a relaxing breath, and close your eyes. Bring to mind and heart the word *anger*. Really fill your whole self with the word *anger,* and begin to notice how you feel physically and emotionally. Take a moment to experience *anger* in every part of you, and notice what colors and ideas come to mind. After you've fully experienced the energy of *anger,* take a deep breath, and let *anger* go with your exhalation.

With your next breath, bring in the word *peace*. Completely take *peace* into every part of you, noticing how your body and energy respond. Repeat the word *peace* again. Notice the colors you sense, as well as the emotions you feel when you are filled up with the energy of *peace*.

Again, it's easy to see the very different energies that two words can carry. Besides the likely agitation you might have felt emotionally and physically with the word *anger,* you may have also recalled some of the events and people who have angered you in the past. Of course, the color most strongly cross-sensed with *anger* is red. Even the phrase "seeing red" is used to describe *anger*.

Along with the color red, *anger* and other harsh emotional words also carry hard, sharp, and spiked energy, not unlike daggers, arrows, and swords. But softer, emotionally embracing words tend to express softer, rounder, more yielding energy. With the word *peace* your body may have softened, too. The most likely colors related to the word *peace* vary from blues to mild green to soft pink. What colors did you experience?

As you continue to work with words, you'll find that their colors are as important as the other sensations you perceive. Yes, red may be the natural vibration of heated, angry confrontational words; but it is also the color of speed, energy, and action. (Even red collection boxes receive more donations than other colors. And red cars are stopped by the police more frequently than any other color.) Clearly red can lift the energy level in many ways—for beneficial and not-so-beneficial results. Knowing how to *decrease* or *increase* red energy by knowing the words that carry red energy—as well as that of other colors—will provide immeasurable power in certain circumstances. (See Appendix 2 for more on colors.)

Shape and Form

Although the shapes and forms of words aren't quite as significant and influential as the other energies words carry, it's important to take a look at them—literally!

A large majority of people tend to be more visual than audial—as evidenced by the fact that most magazines are composed predominantly of pictures. That is why people "see" images when they read a book. But beyond the imagination, there is a strong visual impact to words themselves. Take a few moments to look at the following word, and notice how you perceive it:

S p a c e

If you're like most people, you immediately—and even pleasantly—connected with an expansive feeling of *space*. Now, you may think that your experience of that expansiveness was due entirely to the meaning of the word *space*. But take a moment to focus on the next visual: "space." It's the same word with a very different feeling.

Enclosed by quotation marks and text, this image of space just doesn't seem that expansive. Even though the meaning hasn't changed at all, the way you see it informs the way you feel it. This shows two things: how powerful your focus is, and how strongly the format of the written word impacts you. After all, would you rather be this close to a loved one or thisclose?

Depth Perception—Planting the Power

Words like *small, inch,* or *space* teach a great deal about the energies of words. And so do *soft, hard, anger, peace,* and any other word that can come to mind. Knowing the many powerful energies that words carry and how profoundly they influence you is the first step in using Power Words in all the different facets of your life. After all, a word can't be a Power Word unless you know its power.

So start to become more conscious of all the words you think and say. Open yourself to perceiving the real depth of their meaning and energy. Once you've discovered that, you can start using Power Words to trigger action that will get bigger and better results than you can possibly imagine.

Chapter 4

TAKING ACTION
WITH WORDS

*"The right word blazes out at us. Whenever we come upon one of
these intensely right words . . . the resulting effect is physical
as well as spiritual and electrically prompt."*

— MARK TWAIN

The right word does blaze out! Your whole language is a flowing
current of power that moves constantly. It sparks impulses
through your mind, your energy, your life, and into the world. It
never stops, but you can direct it in a way that your responses—
and the world's—actually do become "electrically prompt."

Triggering a New Perspective Changes Everything

All words will determine your perspective, and using new
words helps to give you a new perspective. Most situations can't
be changed entirely with just a word. For instance, when you
used the word *abdominals* to pick up an object, it didn't change
the fact that you had to pick it up. It just changed how you did it.
Whenever you use the word *abdominals,* your focus will change
and so will the outcome—that of using the right posture; having a
strong, supportive core; and picking up your item without injury.

**When situations are challenging, changing your words
will change your energy and your approach,
and that will change your outcome.**

I am reminded of a story about a paratrooper in World War II in the Battle for the Rhine, one of the major battles of the war. Before he parachuted from the plane, he found himself silently and fearfully asking, *What am I doing here?*

Then, some part of himself deep inside answered, *Why are you thinking that? This is a daring adventure!* With this, his fear was eased, and a new perspective was gained. He went into the battle in a more ready, less rigid state. And he came out of the battle, and the war, alive.

Did this new perspective, these new words, help to save this man's life? Who's to say? His electrically prompt responses certainly became more daring. But using the right word not only molds your reality with its meaning; it lifts your energy and sends your message unencumbered to the world. Did the world get the message that he was less vulnerable? Perhaps so.

Now, of course, most people would be doubtful, intimidated, and frightened out of their minds if they found themselves in such a life-or-death situation. Who wouldn't be? Though the Battle for the Rhine was successful in terms of the ground won, it cost over 65 percent of the lives of the airborne forces. It was a frightening and horrifying event. But this story illustrates how dramatically the words you say to yourself can alter your attitude, perspective, and your actions. It's not that this man was excited about going into battle, but he used words that made it less fearful for him. The situation of the war hadn't changed, and his position within it hadn't changed. Only the words changed—and, consequently, so did his emotional response, his energy, and his approach.

And this can happen for you, too. No matter what you're facing—whether it's frightening or just plain dull—you an change your experience of it with a word.

Your Daring Adventure

Take a moment to think of the rest of your day. Don't start to itemize the things you have to do; just think about your day. Now close your eyes and say to yourself *daring adventure!* Feel this energy fill you, and say these words again. You can feel your own energy stir as you apply these words to your day. Even your old tasks seem to become new. There could be a discovery around any corner! And throughout your day, all you have to do is say *daring adventure* to yourself, and even the most mundane tasks fill you with an exhilarating sense of *adventure!*

So you see, even when a situation can't be changed, what is thought and said about it can be. The new words bring new definitions and associations that apply new forces and energies.

Another great reason to use Trigger Words—and phrases like *daring adventure*—is how quick and easy they are! Brief, ubiquitous, easy to recall, and readily available—words can be used frequently, instantly focusing your energy and often delivering immediate results. This succinct immediacy can be more powerful and rapid than the full sentences of affirmations. I've been a proponent of affirmations for many, many years, and I've used them regularly myself. But Power Words have become my go-to method to alter my focus and tap into energy anytime and anywhere.

Less Really Is More: Power Words vs. Affirmations

In a very literal way, Power Words—and even Power Phrases—are *less* than affirmations since they are actually fewer words. And because of this, they can be much easier to remember and to use.

It's been discovered that most people, when given a choice, are more willing to do things that are less demanding and easier to handle. In a study done by Richard Wiseman testing this theory, charity boxes marked "Every Penny Helps" collected more money than those boxes marked "Every Dollar Helps." It seems that those people who didn't want to give a dollar or more ended up giving nothing. While those who were "asked" to do less, did more! If *every penny* helps more, wouldn't it also be true that *every word* would help more, too? Just think about how many times you could say a word in comparison to how many times you're likely to remember to say an affirmation.

Power words are your opportunity to do more and more in many little increments. In this way, less really is more. Since Power Words are easy to recall, simple, and short, you're more likely to use them more frequently throughout your day and your life. Giving them more frequency also gives them more power and ultimately more truth for you. With Power Words you aren't just adding a sentence or two here and there—you're creating the intention and action of using only words that empower, catalyze, and enrich. Using Power Words throughout your day provides thread after thread of action that creates the very fabric of your life and your world.

Affirming Word Power

Think of an affirmation that you might regularly say or read. Take a moment to change that into a simple phrase or word. You don't have to use the same words from the affirmation; use any word or phrase that captures the essence of your affirmation.

For instance, the affirmation *I create forgiveness every day* can be changed to *Forgive!* Or, *I live in a state of love and joy* can become *Joy now!* Notice how each calls you to action the very moment you use them. Take a moment to determine what word or short phrase you could use to replace your affirmations. Say it to yourself and feel the force of it.

Put this word or phrase on an index card, and take it with you over the next week. Also, put the word in several places that you can see. Use the word frequently throughout each day for a week. Notice the difference you feel between affirmations and words—in how often you use them and the impact they make.

I gave this experiment to a number of my classes, and the students found that they used the words much more frequently than the affirmations. I also use the practice of putting words on cards for my clients, so they can bring their psychological discovery more often into their active daily lives, which is where the real changes are made.

Don't think that I'm recommending that you relinquish affirmations—or that affirmations have no value. Affirmations are very powerful tools for change and manifestation. You will find a number of triggering declarations and commands in this book that look and sound just like affirmations.

A declaration is a whole sentence and is used in those situations when a single word or phrase isn't quite sufficient in making the strongest impact. But if a declaration is a complete sentence, then why isn't it an affirmation? Isn't it just a question of semantics? Not at all.

There is a difference between affirmations and declarations. One is a statement that affirms a condition and the other declares a fact and triggers action of body, mind, feeling, and imaging.

To make an affirmation a declaration, you need to really see it, feel it in your heart and body, and *do* it. Don't just say, *I am filled with loving-kindness.* Declare it! Let it trigger that action immediately. Command, *loving-kindness now* and actually create it. Take a deep breath, turn your attention inward, and feel loving-kindness swell and move within you.

You can make every affirmation a declaration by turning it into an action of body, mind, and heart. You can fill your language with words that trigger action and direct your life in a new way. (See more about declarations, commands, and proclamations in Part II.)

Getting Out of Inertia and Triggering Action!

There's a simple word that can spark an immediate response of activity. It's a Trigger Word and command all rolled into one. Everybody has some image, memory, or idea of what goes on behind the scenes on a movie set. The director shouts "Action!" and immediately the scene—along with everyone in it—comes to life. This image is so very common that it's been burned into the cultural mind as a permanent reference. It's always simple, and it's always the same. A director yells "Action!" and people jump.

Well, you're the director in your life, and you can use this Trigger Word to equal effect. You can make yourself jump to action, no matter what you're doing or want to start—from balancing your checkbook, to weeding your garden, to writing a play, to working on your computer. Regardless of the activity, whenever you hesitate to take action, or your energy starts to wane, or you get distracted from your purpose, simply use this command. You'll find—no matter if the task is creative, tedious, or anything in between—that this word will help you put your foot on the gas when procrastination or inertia sets in.

Word Power for Action

Close your eyes and see yourself engaged in an activity you regularly do—or something new you would like to start. Really put yourself there. Then imagine yourself getting distracted, starting to procrastinate, slowing down, or even stopping completely.

Now, take a deep breath, and say to yourself the command word *Action!* Let yourself hear it in your mind, just as you would in the movies. Again, you say, *Action!* Notice that you feel a surge in energy. Your focus immediately returns, and you get back to the task before you. No longer inert, you are filled with energy and purpose—happy to take *Action!*

I have a client, Rita, in New York City who was a grad student and a professor's assistant at Columbia. One of her tasks as assistant was to help grade tests. She really didn't like this duty, and she procrastinated every time—landing her in hot water with the professor. Once she learned the *Action!* Trigger Word, she was really able to get a better jump on her duties. Being a film student, she connected strongly to that word's energy. But you don't have to be a film student to take *Action!*

Determine, now, to use this Trigger Word the next time you find yourself procrastinating when starting or doing any task. Just close your eyes, and say *Action!* Feel the energy of action filling you when you hear that command. You'll immediately get into the action with renewed force, purpose, and determination. Your body and mind will *want* to respond to your command of *Action!* Each time you use this powerful trigger, you'll find that it really does take you instantly back to your purpose.

There have been times when my mind has been wildly distracted, and I had to repeat this Power Word more than a few times. If that happens to you, don't worry. The image of people jumping to action in response to that command has been set in the popular zeitgeist. Say *Action!* as many times as you need to come back to your purpose. This powerful undercurrent of energy will support you and bring you back .

Action! happens to be one of my favorite Power Words, and it certainly is one of those that I use most often. Believe it or not, I sometimes even say *Action!* when my mind starts to wander during meditation. It brings me back to my focus and to the action of meditating right away!

There are lots of other great Trigger Words that are very effective, too. A right word exists for just about any purpose, and you'll find many options in this book. Now get ready to learn the recipe for Trigger Words. Then you'll be able to use them in the most effective way and create them for yourself.

Chapter 5

THE RECIPE TO TRIGGER POWER

*"A word . . . represents a mental presence or energy;
by it something is produced, crystallized, in the mind."*

— JOSEPH CAMPBELL

While every word has power, only some will be utilized to trigger specific results. Later we'll look into the enormous results that Lifting Words can have in your life, bringing consciousness, enthusiasm, will, and love to everything you think or say. But now it's time to learn how to use specific words as tools. Each and every job requires its own unique tool, and you can use Trigger Words for the many jobs you have. But what are the qualities that make these special words stand apart from other words and do their specific jobs so well?

In the labs at Duke University, J.B. Rhine, J.G. Pratt, and their colleagues spent many years researching mind, matter, psychology, and parapsychology. Some of their tests also measured what conditions influenced their participants' success. Emotional investment on the part of the test subjects was at the top of the list. It seems that caring about the testing procedures and their results significantly impacted their performance. The possibility of a reward, the novelty of the material, and even the presence of competition were some of the things that helped the subjects care more—and succeed more.

Some of these influences will help you succeed with Trigger Words, too—especially emotional engagement and novelty. Of course, the reward you gain will happen when you succeed in each endeavor. There's certainly no better incentive than that. Let's take a close look at the six components that help to turn a word into a power tool:

1. Belief

2. Emotional Engagement

3. Novelty and Interest

4. Focus and Meaning

5. Frequency and Repetition

6. A Call to Action—Will and Intention

1. Belief

The greater belief you have, the greater the impact your Power Words and phrases will make. This doesn't only refer to the belief that you have in the word or in the process, but also—and perhaps even more important—the belief you have in yourself.

Belief is a vital aspect in words of prayer, too. Studies show that prayer makes a successful impact in healing. But some of the participants had greater belief in the prayers of others than in their own prayers. (We'll look at the power of healing prayers in Part III.)

Since you will be the one using Power Words, your belief in your own power needs to coincide with your belief in the energy of the word itself. There may be times when your belief in yourself may be lacking, but don't worry. You can start to use the word *believe* as a Trigger Word. When you use it, declare your *belief* in yourself and your words. Then use more and more Power Words throughout your life. Once you start triggering *belief* and increasing your power vocabulary, your stock will go sky high!

I have a client, Anna Rose, whose belief in herself was sorely lacking because of an extended toxic relationship. The word *believe* didn't have much energy for her because she couldn't relate it to herself. I asked her to recall in her history what was her best memory of the word *believe*. She went all the way back to her childhood and recalled with great delight the story of Peter Pan and Tinker Bell. Tinker Bell had been ill, but her inner lights started twinkling as she got stronger and stronger, healed with the energy of *belief*. From that moment on, whenever Anna Rose used the Trigger Word *believe,* she sensed the energy of *belief*—like starlight twinkling inside her. And each time she smiled with delight. After a while, her *belief* in herself grew and grew so much, her career and her relationships almost seemed to twinkle, too!

2. Emotional Engagement

The element of emotional caring produces success. First, care about yourself enough to put Power Words everywhere in your life. Then, of course, you must care about your words, too—all of your words—whether they're meant for your general language or to help with specific purposes.

Like a little shot of verbal caffeine, Trigger Words are meant to incite your actions. In order to do that, they must engage you emotionally in some way. If you don't care about the words you're using, they won't motivate you. Nor will you continue to use them.

Being emotionally invested doesn't mean that you have to choose only words that you love or that are familiar parts of your personal history. Emotional engagement must be balanced with novelty. Sometimes, if you use a Trigger Word too often or for too long, it can start to lose its energy and emotional impact for you. When that happens, it's time to choose an alternate word or phrase so that you can increase the novelty and reinvigorate your interest. You can go back to the earlier word after a while.

3. Novelty and Interest

> *"But nothing lasts, and men are men,*
> *and novelty, by definition, has its day."*
>
> — GYLES BRANDRETH

The Power Words you choose must be interesting to you—and must remain so. There are some words that may never lose their impact, either because of their universal history or their history with you, but these are in the minority. Most words that you use frequently will not remain novel and interesting to you forever. Even the most unique words or phrases can begin to bore you after a time. And if you're bored, you won't continue the practice of using Power Words. Or, if you do, the words that become boring won't carry the same energy they had before. They'll cease to be Power Words and will simply become words.

Of course, just because a Trigger Word needs to maintain its novelty doesn't mean it can't be a familiar or even simple word. Here are a few very simple Trigger Words that I use in irksome situations where negative words seem to be the first that spring to mind. I simply give myself the command, *Good Word* or—to put it another way—*Bon mot* (pronounced "bohn mōe").

Good Word Power

Close your eyes and imagine yourself in the midst of a confrontation, dealing with a frustrating problem, or in a situation that gets your ire up. Really put yourself there, and recall the irritating energy. Think of some of the words that would start coming up for you. Let these words fill your mind now.

Now say the command to yourself, *Good word, good word! Bon mot!* Then immediately find a good word to say—and feel—any good word at all. It could simply be *calm, good, tolerance, joy*—whatever comes to mind. Your *good word* will release the negative pressure. And instead of saying and feeling bad, you can wrap this event and any situation with *good.*

Now, bring *good word* together with another command word. Say *Resolve, resolve, resolve.* Feel it direct you to create a resolution through kindness, understanding, and *good words.*

It's good to have *good words* at the ready. You'll find a list of elevating lifting words in Part IV and Appendix 1, but you could make your own list, too. *Good word* is a simple but very effective trigger because it immediately turns your perspective, intention, and language to good.

Good word is a wonderful example of how everyday words can be used as Trigger Words, but even these will sometimes need to be changed to keep the novelty high. I often change up my Trigger Words by using different languages—foreign words that carry the same or a similar meaning. If the phrase *good word* is too mundane for you, you can change it up with *bon mot,* like I do. It's fun; it's festive; it's French. And it means—of course—*good word!* (You'll find more foreign Trigger Words in Part III.)

You can use any language to alternate a Trigger Word—French, Spanish, Latin. It doesn't matter what language you use, as long as you keep your interest level high. Some words may hold your interest forever. Some will not. After a time, if you find a word losing its impact or making you bored, file it away and choose an alternative.

Whatever new Trigger Word you use in its place needs to be different enough to make it special again—but not so different that you find it confusing, emotionless, or hard to remember. So, don't use any jibberish words unless you have a pleasant and powerful history attached to them. Bottom line: **Your Trigger Words need to be easy to remember, pleasant to say, and inspiring to feel.** And after you've used an alternative for a while, you can come back to the original. When you do, you'll be amazed at how much energy and meaning it has for you again.

4. Focus and Meaning

Trigger Words help you apply certain energies to specific situations. Although some trigger a spontaneous response, when you focus on the energy of the word and on its deeper meaning, it will increase its power and impact.

As you've already seen in many of our processes, *taking a deep breath* when using a Trigger Word is a body signal to center yourself, open your senses, and pursue a certain directive of mind and body. Don't just recite the word; take a moment to fully feel the profound, deeper meaning and energy of it. Even with simple words, the more you deeply hold the meaning, the more you will be able to channel that energy. So every time you say a Trigger Word, don't just say it; feel its meaning inside you and all the way through you.

5. Frequency and Repetition

"All our talents increase in the using, and every faculty, both good and bad, strengthens by exercise."

— ANNE BRONTË

You're going to be using words all your life, so you might as well be applying their great force for the good they can do. Frequent repetition in your use of Power Words strengthens your command of their power. This frequent practice actually trains your brain to look for and direct the energy in any given moment or situation. Even when you're feeling low and your energy is flagging, with repetition you can make more headway than you think.

Imagine you're trying to drive a nail with a hammer, but you're feeling too tired or sore to put much energy into it. What would you have to do? It's simple. You'd just have to repeat the action a little more frequently to drive the nail home. Trigger Words work in much the same way. The more frequently you use a word, the more you'll drive that intention home. The other by-product of frequency and repetition is how much they build your belief in yourself and in your power. So keep repeating and repeating. And if you're ever feeling weak and you start to doubt, don't falter. Keep hammering away with your Power Words, and you'll succeed beyond measure!

6. A Call to Action—Will and Intention

Many Trigger Words are calls to action. They voice your will. And your energy becomes aligned to their meaning and their force.

This call to action doesn't only refer to literal action. It can be physical, mental, emotional, or spiritual. The call to action can trigger activity of the body, mental focus on a task, emotional forgiveness, heightened awareness, calming feelings, new efforts in communication, or a variety of other actions.

Here's a Trigger Word that I have taught to my clients to help break defeating patterns—whether they are patterns of behavior, thought, or feeling. You can give it a try yourself. Whether you find yourself starting—or deeply engaged in—a negative train of thought, a downward emotional spiral, or a sabotaging physical behavior, you can *override* that action with just a word.

Word Power Override

Close your eyes and think of a deflating or defeating habit you have—in thought, feeling, or deed. It doesn't have to be extreme in nature. It's just one of the patterns you'd like to set aside.

Imagine yourself caught up in one of those moments. See yourself there completely. Let yourself feel stuck—again—really stuck in this sabotaging action. Now take a deep breath, sit up a bit straighter, and slowly say to yourself, *Override, override, override.* With another deep breath, you immediately feel a new power and determination to *override* this habitual action or thought. You get a jolt of energy, and you sense the great potential as you *override* this pattern. Whenever you say *override,* you can immediately change what you're doing. And you celebrate not being controlled by that pattern any longer.

Override is an effective word to stop an automatic pattern in is tracks because it's technical in nature. It throws a cog in the wheel of old thought patterns and interrupts them long enough for you to direct yourself to new thoughts. It confuses the moment just enough to open the door to a new way.

I shared the Trigger Word *override* with a friend, Fred, who had suffered with bouts of depression off and on throughout his adult life. He used the Trigger Word *override* and found that it had an immediate effect for him—bringing him out of his depression, stimulating him to choose different thoughts right away. Now he uses *override,* and it helps him *override* his depression every time.

There are some defeating patterns that can be very deeply entrenched, and you might have to redo this process and repeat *override* a number of times—especially when you find yourself in the throes of long-term sabotaging thoughts or behaviors.

Although you can also use *disengage, shift, change, detach,* or *release* for some of the alternates, *override* is my go-to word. Whether you're just reaching for a second piece of pie or submerged in a sea of victimization, you can *override* that habit with this Trigger Word. *Override* is one of those perfect words that helps you do exactly what it means. (We'll see more about other ways to override strong emotional patterns in Chapter 9.)

The Perfect Word

*"The difference between a perfect word and near-perfect word
is like the difference between lightning and a lightning bug."*

— MARK TWAIN

The perfect Power Word is the one that works best for you.
There are words that inspire, motivate, compel, or even disgust.
But, just like art, you must decide for yourself what moves you.

Everyone experiences the energy of words differently. If you
were to read a passage in a book that describes a tree-lined street,
the images you perceive would be different from those of any
other person. It's much the same with Trigger Words. Some may
impact other people more than they influence you. Some may
bring you enormous energy while falling flat for others. That's
why I've tried to present so many different words and alternates
throughout this book for you to experience. If one word doesn't
work, try something else. You are the writer of your story; you can
choose the words that you like best.

I also encourage you to be on the lookout for new Trigger
Words that you can find on your own. Whenever you discover
new words, really take the time to experience their energy. That
will help you know how to use them best. Whatever Trigger Words
you choose, make sure that they reflect the positive, the present,
and the powerful. Then allow yourself to immediately follow them
with the precise action and response that each word ignites.

You can make your life an exciting exploration for new words.
They're lurking everywhere—in novels, dictionaries, television
shows, plays, and even in everyday conversations. Sometimes
they'll be unique, lyrical, or even poetic. Other times they'll be
common and, at first blush, mundane—like the phrase *good word.*
You'll find that the words that trigger action to change your life
are all *good words.* So keep expanding the list of words that light
you up, and soon you'll be lighting up the world.

TRIGGER
WORDS FOR
EVERY PURPOSE

"Words are like planets, each with its own gravitational pull."

— KENNETH BURKE

Chapter 6

WORDS AT WORK, HOME, AND PLAY

"Words may be deeds."

— A ESOP

Y ou can use specific words to align with actions that you already do on a daily basis. But Trigger Words can also help to spark action where there may have been none before. They can help trigger a response in so many situations—from cleaning up your clutter, sparking creativity, eating for better health, dealing with difficult people, getting a good night's sleep, and on and on and on. Whether you're busy at work, spending the day at home, or dining out, you will find dozens and dozens of Power Words in this book to help you. In Chapter 10 you'll see how to combine Trigger Words with activities that you already do every day, but here are a few that you can use to start whole new actions whenever you wish.

Persevering in Work and Relationships

Shakespeare once asked, "Will you persevere to joy?" What a concept—a state of endurance and persistence toward joy! Here's a command trigger for those times when your enthusiasm and industry seem to be waning. It spurs you on like the Trigger Word *Action,* but this time it links that action to joy. Whether you're engaged in something simple or the most important creative endeavor of your life, this trigger can help.

Persevere to Joy

Imagine yourself engaged in some task that lies before you now (and may have done so for quite a while). See yourself becoming weary of it and slacking off. Yet there is a reason for your doing this task. Accomplishing it will please you, and you know it. Close your eyes, take a deep breath, and say to yourself, *Persevere to joy.* Fill yourself with that force, that command. Feel your energy pick up as you really begin to *Persevere to joy* in this task. You become more tireless, diligent, and happy. You even seem to work faster. You're inexhaustible, and nothing discourages you whenever you give yourself the command, *Persevere to joy.*

There are some people at work—and other places, too—who seem to throw a blanket over joy wherever they go. Here's a Power Word that helped a good friend Linda, who, as court recorder, often has to be present at depositions with horrible battling opponents. On one particularly grueling day, Linda would frequently take a deep breath and hold the words, *Bliss, bliss, bliss.* Repeating this Power Word distanced her from what was happening around her and immediately took her to an inner peace. Try this word yourself when you need *Bliss.*

Linda wasn't in a position of influencing the negative, screaming people around her, but there are times when each of us would like to bring some influence to bear in a situation. Yet influence never happens by pushing people around. Maya Angelou once said that people will forget what you say or do, but they'll never forget how you made them feel. The I Ching mirrors that sentiment when it equates the process of influence with wooing. Love, modesty, gentleness, and warmth will all soften a hard heart more than insistence, anger, control, and aggressiveness.

Influence Through Wooing

See yourself in a situation where you have to help others become aware of an important point or helpful suggestion. Close your eyes for a moment and breathe deeply, saying to yourself, *Influence through wooing, influence through love.* You are modest, kind, and warm in your demeanor. You are confident, yet gentle, in your words.

Breathe in the energy of *influence through love* again. And you know that those who won't relinquish their positions cling to them out of fear or vulnerability or closed-mindedness. You reach out a loving hand, a gentle touch. Your sensitivity and love to them are not false—for those who are awake never feel the need to control those who sleep. It is your love that will influence their waking.

Clearing Out of Clutter Canyon

Removing clutter is essential in supporting the highest flow of energy, personal success, and financial abundance in your life. It's imperative not to let things pile up, but we are human after all. If you have boxes, stacks, piles, heaps, and mounds of stuff that you haven't used (or rarely use) in your living or working spaces, it's time to clear it all out.

Blocking beneficial energy flow in your life is just the beginning of clutter's negative effects. It's disruptive and wastes your time looking for things. It prevents you from staying current with your paperwork. It reinforces your attachment to stuff and prohibits your experience of beauty in your daily life. So, buy some file cabinets and storage bins. Organize what you must keep, give away what you can, and throw away the rest.

Of course, you know all this already. But did you know that there are a few powerful phrases that command a new response to staying on top of things? I learned these many years ago, and they have helped me enormously. They have become organizational mantras for me.

File it, don't pile it is actually from the title of a book by Pat Dorff. Many people think that when something is pending, their notes and paperwork have to be left on the desk or else they'll forget about it. In the end, a big bunch of papers dealing with several pending situations end up in a pile. And since all except the one paper on the top is covered, everything below is forgotten . . . but you can learn a new way when you use new words.

Word Power on File

See yourself dealing with your everyday paperwork. Take a deep breath and say to yourself, *File it, don't pile it.* When you do, you *file it* immediately. You create a folder as soon as it's needed. You have one for pending papers that you can check regularly and even have a "To-Do" folder.

From now on, whenever you say the words *File it, don't pile it,* you file what's at hand immediately. And every day you see a clear desk, you have a clear mind and an easier day—because you always *file it.*

Even once you have file folders, you still have to build the habit of using them. And that brings me to the next Power Phrase that I learned many years ago. It helps you take action with your paperwork and your e-mails and texts in the immediate present. It's very easy to remember because it's also an acronym: *Only handle it once* or *OHIO.*

OHIO Word Power

Getting things done feels good. It helps you have a sense of achievement and keeps you from getting behind. All you have to do is remind yourself, *Only handle it once.* Whenever you say, *Only handle it once,* you do each task while it's right at hand. When you have to file a paper, write a letter, make a call, or answer an e-mail, you do it then. As soon as you say, *Only handle it once,* you do. You don't procrastinate and get behind. And you don't feel overwhelmed by what you have to do. You simply say, *Only handle it once.* And you handle it—successfully, easily, and quickly. And it's done.

I have a client, Lewis, who ran his own interior-decorating business that was experiencing a slump in funds. He had a small storefront with furniture and samples of finishes that he kept very orderly and nice looking. His back office, though, was quite another story. Files, papers, receipt books, carpet samples, tiles, catalogs, and drapery samples were laying in so many piles, it was impossible to navigate from the door to the back of the room.

I gave him some organizational tips to get him started and taught him the *File it, don't pile it* and *Only handle it once* triggers, which he found very helpful. He even had them printed, framed, and hung on the wall opposite his desk. Being an interior decorator, Lewis hadn't only studied design, but he had also studied feng shui. Knowing how strongly the flow of energy is connected to the flow of money, he was very highly motivated. He made himself a rule to put every sample back in the sample racks as soon as he was finished with it. And he began to always file away papers, proposals, and receipts. (He had also purchased more file cabinets, which helped.)

Eventually Lewis had everything put away. His Trigger Words helped him build new habits that became cemented in his daily business life. His client list grew, and his income was on the incline. Even more important, running his business was easier, and he was so much happier!

When you do the OHIO process, be sure to visualize yourself taking swift and successful action. Try to come back to this process several times in the next few weeks until you anchor *Only handle it once* as a Trigger Command. Whenever you say it, you snap to quick action and easily finish the task at hand so that you can link the response to the trigger.

With this Trigger Phrase, you'll do things immediately, and you'll begin to put things away *right away*. It takes far less time than always moving piles around or playing hide and seek with your keys, purse, notes, papers, bills, checkbook, and so on. You may have a tendency to misplace one item frequently, or you may find yourself losing lots of things on a regular basis. A person with a chronic pattern of looking for lost objects can end up feeling like a real loser. Think about it; the word loser is a literal description for someone who's often misplacing papers or objects. But it's a description you can easily live without.

Lost or Found?

Close your eyes and take a relaxing breath. Think for a moment about your home or office, and consider how often you have trouble finding misplaced papers, documents, folders, or objects. Think of the word *lost,* and remember how much time you've *lost* in looking for things. Hold the word *lost* inside you, and feel it deeply. Really experience the energy of *lost* inside you, and notice how you feel.

Now, with your next breath, send the word *lost* away from you. Realize that you're not *lost,* nor is anything else in your world. Take another deep breath, and bring the word *found* into your mind and heart. Feel how good it feels to be *found*. Know that everything you seek is *found*. Your power is *found;* your focus and clarity are *found*. Your strength of purpose is *found.* Even your actions for organization are *found.* Whenever you use the Trigger Word *found,* you'll take a deep breath and find clarity, power, and purpose within—and everything you seek outside.

If you want some help finding lost objects, you'll also discover a wonderful, and extraordinarily effective, little invocation that helps you find lost items in Chapter 13. But for now, try this process whenever you seem to lose your power, focus, or clarity in any measure. And if you have too much stuff and clutter, start to clear things away. There may be lots of boxes or piles that need to be tackled, but don't get overwhelmed. Just start with one box. Be patient and diligent, taking care of just one box or pile each day—or even each week. See each new box and each new day as a new start.

"The secret of getting ahead is getting started. The secret of getting started is breaking your complex, overwhelming tasks into small, manageable tasks, and then starting on the first one."

— MARK TWAIN

Ordering Power When You're Out to Lunch

For a lot of people who want to maintain a healthy weight, or who even want to drop a few pounds, eating out can be a real challenge. Here's an old term that gets new meaning as a declaration: *Power Lunch.* From now on, this declaration can trigger the power you want to feel and the action you want to take when you're dining out. It will inspire you to eat a meal that truly empowers.

Word Power on the Menu

Imagine that you're dining out with friends or co-workers. The warm buttered rolls and sugary desserts are beginning to challenge your resolve to choose what's best for you—not just what tastes best.

Close your eyes, take a deep breath, and say to yourself, *Power Lunch*. With another deep breath, you turn your focus inward, and you take in the force and vibration of *power*. You say *Power Lunch* again, and you are filled with the desire to nourish only your *power*. You seem to shine inside with the certainty of taking actions that honor you—actions that feed and nurture your real *power*. You know that this, and every meal, is your *Power Lunch*. And each time you use this phrase, you are filled to the brim and nourished with *power*.

Your Ticket for a Trip to Bountiful

I don't think there's a person on the planet who doesn't want their financial endeavors to succeed and grow. Employees want a raise or bonus. Financiers want an investment to redouble. Movie stars want a blockbuster hit. And farmers want bountiful crops that sell for big money. Of course, there are many types of abundance. (For more see Chapter 21.)

Financial prosperity is important to many. The first requirement for *financial success* is one's effort and actions. Success requires taking action. But since words also carry intentions out to the Universe and make them real in our lives, we can also use Power Words to send forth a reality of abundant success.

To that end, I had long searched for a Power Word or phrase that proclaimed an ever-growing abundance in my life. Though his play is bittersweet, I have always liked Horton Foote's turn of phrase, *a trip to bountiful*. But, as a trigger, these words seem to make *bountiful* a destination to reach rather than a present reality.

Instead I choose terms that indicate *financial abundance* at all times, such as *unceasing bounty; growing wealth; financial prosperity, now and always;* and *incessant increscence.* This is a fun one. It means "unceasing increase . . . in one's possessions or influence." Just the sound of it makes me chuckle! Of all of the great Power Words of abundance, I think my favorite is the French, *Succès fou* (pronounced "sük-sĕ foo"). It means *mad success—crazy, extraordinary financial success.* What fun words!

Bounty Abounds

Think of a financial endeavor that you have pursued and may still be pursuing. You have planted the seeds and taken abundant action, and now you want to send forth your desire for its *abundant success.* Close your eyes and see your *bounty growing,* your bank account getting larger. You deserve to receive all the richness the world can give you.

Take a deep breath and say to yourself *unceasing bounty,* and feel your *abundance* grow. With the command *unceasing bounty,* you renew your commitment to the *abundant action* that creates *abundant wealth.* You say to yourself, *succès fou;* and you breathe in *wild, crazy, financial success.* It is your reality. And you say, *thank you.*

Of course to support financial abundance, make sure there's an investment of abundant right action on your part. Your actions tell the world what you want to make real. Then the world becomes your partner and makes it real with you.

I have a client, Connie, a jewelry maker who did beautiful work. She started to combine the Power Words *abundant wealth* and *abundant action.* Then she started to market her jewelry more, something she hadn't felt comfortable doing before. But *abundant action* didn't just mean creating jewelry to Connie; it also meant financial action, like marketing. And once she took it, she started to receive!

Taking Your Words to Bed

Sometimes it can be difficult to calm your mind as you get ready for sleep—especially after an emotionally charged or busy day. You could be lying there hoping for sleep while your mind races through your plans and all of the fragments of your life. Some people might turn on the television to distract them, but this will only replace the internal chaos with a barrage of external noise, images, and questionable themes that are just as stimulating.

Even at bedtime there is a simple declaration that can take you out of your day and immediately put you into a calm and peaceful state of rest. Within it is an image that gives you an absolute and unfaltering embrace of love. It's a Divine love that penetrates, warms, and fills you with a perfect serenity and peace—just the right thing to prepare you for perfect sleep. When you do this process, be sure the lights and television are turned off.

Sleep at Hand

Once you're in bed, put yourself in a comfortable position. Take a deep breath, and gently declare to yourself, *I rest in the hand of God.* Really visualize this and feel the great, embracing energy of God's love supporting you. Feel it deeply, and snuggle into it. Say again, *I rest in the hand of God.* Burrow down deeper into the covers. Imagine that you really do rest in a great, loving hand that will never let you down.

Feel yourself wrapped and held in the strength, peace, love, and security that are eternal and expansive beyond measure. Softly repeat *I rest in the hand of God* a few more times. Continue to hold this experience in your heart and mind until you gently drift off to sleep, resting in the boundless support of the Divine.

I shared this process on the radio and later received dozens of e-mails from people who added this beautiful trigger to their bedtime habits. One, Ella, told me that her husband had died in a car accident about a year before. Until his death she hadn't slept by herself for over 20 years. She had, of course, been overwhelmed by her grief, but bedtime was the hardest for her. It was when she felt most alone. Once she started to declare, *I rest in the hand of God,* she wasn't alone anymore. Ella knows she will continue to miss her husband, who was her dearest life partner. But now she no longer dreads going to bed because she knows she will sleep in a warm, powerful, and serene embrace.

You can do this whenever you want to rest in greater strength, love, and support. But if you'd rather connect with something other than a Divine personality, you can also practice a similar statement that you can create for yourself, for example: *I sleep with a peaceful heart,* or *I rest in tranquil ease.* These would work fine, too. Or you can choose some part of nature that you find comforting.

I would suggest you give the original a try and reach out to the God of your understanding. For me, after a hectic day in a far too human world, connecting with a higher, Divine presence reminds me of a greater life. I use this trigger almost every night. It creates a beautiful, serene awareness of one's eternal truth and grace. For me, it's like returning to my home in heaven. And there is no better place to end the day, nor better state of mind to carry into tomorrow.

As you can see, Trigger Words can take you from action to rest, and from financial bounty to abundant love and peace. You can put Trigger Words to work with so many different tasks and in so many situations, but you must remember to use them. Just like a treadmill—they can only work for you if you use them!

It's easy to forget things when you're trying to build a new habit. It might help you to put a few of your favorite Power Words on a card to take with you. Glance at it several times a day. Each time you say one of the Trigger Words, use that moment to take a breath and hold that word's energy deep inside you. Power Words are like tools—they're always at hand. And if you use them, they can help you build an extraordinary life.

Chapter 7

COMMANDS AND DECLARATIONS: THE DETERMINED VOICE

"Thou shalt also decree a thing,
and it shall be established unto thee:
And the light shall shine upon thy ways."

— JOB 22:28

There are lots of things we want to do, wish to have, and hope to create. Yet opportunity often seems to slip away. We need to command the moment and proclaim our truth. And we can do both with Power Words.

For most people "having command of their vocabulary" means having a large vocabulary or excelling in a broad use of words. But you can command your vocabulary in a very different way. You can get on top of everything you say and use a commanding language. You'll be amazed at how this gives you a greater command of your life, too.

As you get more practice with Trigger Words, you'll find that some of them act as commands, while others declare and proclaim. Although the words *command, declare,* and *proclaim* are sometimes used as synonyms for each other, there are important distinctions in their meanings.

When used as Trigger Words, they will all evoke an immediate response on your part. Sometimes that response can be physical, sometimes mental, and sometimes emotional. But, regardless of the nature of the response, the intention is to react at once. A Trigger Word that *commands* provides a call to action. A *declaration* is an unshakable statement that something is so—a bit like an affirmation on steroids. And a *proclamation* acts as an even bolder, sometimes more formal shout to the world. *Declarations* and *proclamations* have a stronger emotional involvement than affirmations. So make your affirmations *declarations*. Even just defining them as such will give them more power for you and for the world.

Now let's look at *commands, declarations,* and *proclamations* individually.

Taking Command

The word *command* comes from the Latin *mandare,* which meant *to entrust, to put in one's hand,* or *to commit.* These original meanings seem a bit softer than today's definitions, *to give an order* or *to direct with authority,* but as we use Trigger Words, it is the stronger sense of *command* that we want to harness.

To take command of your life, you have to put commands in your language—not commands of others, but words that command *you* to act, to think, to be who you want to be, and to do what you want to do.

Trigger Words that call you to action add a dynamic quality to your life. Using them with any regularity can make a great impact. It puts you in a state of readiness to act—and readiness to embrace every opportunity that comes your way. When you're more at the ready and willing to act, you're less likely to waste time ruminating, doubting, overanalyzing, and hesitating.

One of the words that gets a lot of airtime in the attempt to stimulate action is *should.* The word *should* lacks a sense of desire, so it doesn't really trigger action. *Should* carries only a sense of obligation, laborious duty, and even guilt. If you're going to do anything—even out of "have to" or obligation (such as going to work or even cleaning the house)—erase all *shoulds* and determine why you *desire* and *choose* to do such a thing. *(I appreciate the money and support this job brings to my life. I enjoy my house being tidy, and I know it helps the flow of good energy in my life.)*

Should is very low in energy and doesn't really motivate at all. *Should* just tends to make us feel guilty when we don't have to be. Commanding Trigger Words are much more demonstrative. They stimulate immediate action and make you feel more powerful.

A Little Word—Big Command

Here's a word that you'll remember from Chapter 2. You were able to sense its energy as a word very easily. Even though you weren't using it as a Trigger Word, it still elicited a very distinctive response. It's the word *tall*. And when you use it as a command, it will literally make you stand taller.

I bet you couldn't possibly remember the countless times that you've told yourself, *I should improve my posture,* or the times your parents told you, "Sit up straight." When you say *you should,* it probably causes only a small and temporary response. And although your parents probably got you to sit up straight when you were a kid, now those words only make you feel like you're being scolded. Here's a technique that can help you get rid of this *should* once and for all.

Word Power for a Tall Order

Close your eyes and simply notice your body. Slowly say the word *tall* in your mind. Take a deep breath as you say *tall* again, filling yourself with the energy of *tall*. Notice as your shoulders seem to pull back, your spine straightens, and you're body aligns. You are *taller, straighter,* and *stronger*. And now you know that *tall* is no longer just a word; it's an intention, a desire, a command. Every time you say the word *tall* to yourself or aloud, you will immediately stand straighter, and you'll feel yourself to be the tallest person in the room—confident, powerful, and strong. From now on, the command *tall* instantaneously lifts you to new heights—in body, mind, and spirit!

I taught this command to a friend, Len, who is a teacher in a very tough inner-city high school. Len is a trim, confident 6'4" man with excellent posture; so why would he even need to use the Trigger Word *tall?* Well, even for the confident, the task of dealing with the intractable, incorrigible, and downright defiant can get you down, literally and figuratively. During those times, Len uses the command *tall,* and he immediately feels more assured, and even bigger! He stands straighter, and his voice even gets deeper. He told me that feeling taller makes him feel more formidable. He doesn't get meaner; he just gets stronger. He can handle the day—and the students—with greater ease. And the students, who can feel the energy, handle him with greater respect.

Command the Connection

Everybody has those times when what's happening at hand seems to take precedence over the people who matter. Sometimes your kids, friends, spouse, parents, co-workers, or others are in need of your attention. And your first response—at that moment at least—is to brush them away so you can get back to what's on your plate. Sometimes you could even find yourself talking with these people, nodding and responding, while your focus is really somewhere else.

This is a human condition that happens to everyone. But the love and honoring of relationships requires a real presence in the little moments and the large. And you will know a deeper connection in the long run when you really connect in the here and now. Here is a Trigger Word that you can use when, like me, you get distracted from those who are present.

Engaging Word Power

Close your eyes and imagine that someone who needs your attention comes up to you during a very busy time. It seems like a bother at first, but you stop what you're doing. Taking a deep breath, you say to yourself the word *engage*. Immediately, your eyes connect. You are fully and deeply aware of what this person is sharing with you. You are *engaged*.

If you become distracted by thoughts of what you have to do, you simply repeat to yourself the word *engage*. It reconnects you happily, purposefully, and instantly.

From now on, whenever you need to immediately connect with anyone, you simply say to yourself, *engage*. And you do.

These are just a few of the Trigger Words that can act as commands. There are several throughout this book, but you can use your own if you'd prefer. And don't forget to keep the novelty—and therefore your interest and involvement—high.

For instance, you can use the words *big, height,* or even *to the clouds!* to alternate with *tall.* For some reason, the immediate effect of the word *tall* never seems to wear off for me—no matter how often I use it. It's so effective for me, my body reacts the very second I even think about using the word *tall.* I sometimes use *to the clouds!* because it's fun, and it reminds me to lift my mind to a loftier place while getting taller at the same time. If you find that a certain Trigger Word continues to work for you, even after a long time, it's not necessary to change it, but it is fun to mix it up a little.

You can choose from a number of alternatives for *engage. Connect* and *link* are a few. Be creative with command words. Pick any word you'd like for whatever action you'd like to take. Use demonstrative words, or words that carry energy that really moves you. As Joseph Conrad says, "Command is a strong magic." But a commanding word doesn't hypnotize you or force you; it moves you. That's its magic.

You can also use commanding statements whenever any situation calls for it. Recently, I wanted to find a quote from a section of the I Ching called "The Gentle Penetrating Wind." I was in a hurry and didn't want to take time looking for it. I picked up the book, made the command for that section, and opened it to that very page. I also remember a certain conversation I had with my friend Jeanie. I was recommending a book, but I couldn't remember the name of the author. In the old days I would have said, "OMG, I'm forgetting everything." But as soon as I started that statement, I caught myself and commanded, *I must remember now!* And the name popped into my mind immediately. Now whenever I start to forget, I make the command to remember. And usually I do!

You can work with any statement, phrase, or word that commands whatever response you might require. Discover the words and phrases that direct you with their meaning and energy. And use them throughout in your life—both in your actions and your declarations to the world.

I Declare!

The word *declaration* comes from the Latin *clarare,* which means *to make clear.* A declaration strongly asserts what's so. And all of your words, actions, and even your feelings are declarations to yourself and to the world.

There is a little test you can use to determine the impact of the statements you make. I call it the *declaration test.* If you ever wonder if something is what you really want to say, just put the words *I declare* before it. You'll be able to truly discover the weight your words carry to the world.

Declaring More Than What Is

"It is what it is," may arguably be one of the most often used observations in the world today. It might be considered a declaration because it certainly does make a statement of what's so. After all, nothing could ever be what it isn't. But it doesn't declare the speaker's involvement, intention, or response. The statement "It is what it is" only *implies* a possible state of acceptance of things as they are. But if you really want to declare that you're letting go of control and even detaching, it might be good to use words that say that more precisely.

Now, it's a great and wonderful thing when you don't allow yourself to be upset and buffeted about by circumstances around you. Saying, "It is what it is," may be a good start, but it may not be as precise as declaring, "I accept this as it is," Or "I'm letting this go." So, the next time this statement comes to mind, think about changing it up a bit. Declare to the world that however things are, you're letting go.

Word Power That Lets Go

Close your eyes, and think of a time when you might have said, "It is what it is." It might have been a challenging situation, an event out of your control, a missed opportunity, or a disappointment of some kind. Take a deep breath, and say to yourself, *I accept this. I'm letting go.* Smile, and relax into a state of easy *acceptance* and detaching.

Gently repeat, *I accept this. I'm letting go.* In the great scheme of things—however things are—it's still okay. You're still okay. Feel the peace and freedom you sense in *letting go.* And whenever you say this, you declare your release to the world. You accept and you *let go.*

You can try different languages, too. You can use the French *da rien* (pronounced "deh REE-en"), which means "It's nothing," or "Nothing important." Or you can use other replacements: *I'm happy to let this go, I surrender the outcome, I'm free of this worry,* or even *Joyful detachment now.* There's a wonderful diversity in words, so select the declarations that mean the most to you. And if you'd like, you can take this situation and this sentiment in a whole different direction by declaring, "It will go well." (See Chapter 11 for this declaration and for more details in using foreign words as Power Words.)

I like to use *It matters not,* because it takes me even more deeply into the act of detachment. I really make an effort at living life in the process, not in the outcomes. And this little sentiment helps to keep me from getting too tangled up in my expectations—though there are occasions when I need to repeat it more than a few times! It also acts as a reminder not only to detach from outer situations, but also to find my foundation and strength within.

Because I use *It matters not* so frequently, I change it up by using a different language. The German is just two simple words: *Machts nichts* (pronounced "mahx nix").

It Matters Not

Think of those times when you find yourself far too entangled in your expectations. You may be so embroiled in your desired outcomes that you're defining your well-being through them rather than through yourself.

Take a deep breath and close your eyes now. Think of this situation and say the command, *It matters not.* As you do, you are instantly reminded that external matters are just illusions, and your truth and power belong to your internal reality. With another cleansing breath, say *Machts nichts, It matters not,* again. And let yourself feel the exquisite deliverance from being defined solely by events in a limited, temporary, material world.

Proclamations

If a declaration is stronger than an observation, a proclamation is much stronger still. The word *proclamation* comes from the Latin *clamare,* which means *to cry out,* and which is also the same root word for *clamor, a loud outcry* or *noise.* It is a public statement—an announcement or broadcast of your words to the world.

Your proclamations demonstrate a desire to express a stronger will with a broader reach. It's possible—and often beneficial—to ratchet up a declaration into a proclamation. Let's take a look.

"A ship in the harbor is safe—but that is not what ships are for."

— JOHN A. SHEDD

Sometimes life can feel like being on a ship tossed about and torn apart on a stormy sea. During these times it's natural to want to retreat to safe harbor. But safe harbor doesn't take us to broader horizons. Indeed, the word *safe* can actually carry an underlying meaning of retreat, needing protection, or even hiding. In Chapter 11 you'll see how to trigger *courage* to break through hesitance, but some situations call for even more. During the *storms of life,* staying safe may feel like, well, the safest thing to do, but what's really required is nothing less than the proclamation: *Fearless.*

Fearless Word Power

Close your eyes and think for a moment about a situation or time when you were feeling vulnerable or frightened. Remember it now, and begin to say the word *safe* to yourself. As you hold the word *safe* inside you, notice what happens to your energy and your body. It might be assuring to feel *safe,* but do you also, perhaps, feel somehow smaller or meeker?

You might even feel like you're retreating or backing into a hiding place, under the covers, or into a corner. Of all the things you feel with *safe,* notice that taking action is not a part of that experience.

Now, take a deep breath, and with your exhalation let *safe* go. Pull into your mind, your heart, and your whole body the word *fearless*. Fill yourself with the energy of *fearless*. Notice what happens to your own energy as you proclaim *fearlessness* to the world. The situation hasn't changed, but you've changed. You're *fearless,* and you feel bigger, bolder, more daring, and ready to approach any difficulty. Know that whenever you make the proclamation *fearless* in the future, you really are, and you take the action that shows it.

I shared this process and the proclamation *fearless* with a client, Alice, who was getting behavioral treatment for various phobias, including agoraphobia. She had so many different fears that there were many times she kept herself home because of them. With a fear of highly populated places and driving over bridges, highways, and heights, her world kept getting smaller and smaller. But she wanted a full life with her husband and children.

She began to add the proclamation *fearless* any time she had a panic attack. She told me that it helped give her the power not to hide "in safety" anymore. She began to take more command of her language and her actions, venturing farther and farther to the places that used to make her hide. She really did become *fearless*— and very busy traveling to exciting destinations with her family!

There's little that can stop you when you *command* your actions, *declare* your truth, and *proclaim* what you want to make real. Many of the other Power Words in this book *command* and *declare*, so be open to their dynamic intentions. You can also proclaim your intention to make successful and easy decisions simply by using word power.

I Can't Decide

These are words that you should refrain from using as much as possible. Declaring a state of indecisiveness will perpetuate it, but you can make a different command.

Deciding Now

Think of a decision that has you wavering. Let go of any inclination that you're unable to decide. Close your eyes and make the command *Deciding now.* Take a deep breath and fill yourself with this *decisive energy. Decide now,* and notice the first response that comes to mind.

Take another deep breath and let that all go. Now say the Trigger Words, *destiny decision.* Fill yourself with the energy that there is one choice—one answer—in this decision that is your *destiny.* What is it?

If someone told you that you had no choice, this is the option or outcome that you would fight to regain. This is the choice that compels you. It is your *destiny.* See it now.

There are lots of different techniques in using word energy to help you make your choices. Turn the page to find out what they are.

Chapter 8

MAKING DECISIONS WITH WORD ENERGY

"Destiny is not a matter of chance, it is a matter of choice."

— WILLIAM JENNINGS BRYAN

At first blush, most of life's choices don't seem like life or death decisions. Yet, every decision—even those little ones you make day in and day out—will impact your life. Indeed, the little choices made over and over again can have a greater impact than any other.

Sometimes certain choices are quite clear, so clear that there wouldn't be any doubt or even a moment's hesitation. There are other decisions, however, that can be polarizing—making you so ambivalent that you ruminate about it for days, weeks, or even months—and you often end up making no decision at all.

There are lots of different strategies that can help you make decisions. You can consult with experts. You can create the ever-popular pro and con list. You can make a determination based on personal or financial needs. You can talk to family and friends. And, beyond all this, you can use word energy to better inform yourself about your choices.

You've already been experiencing the different types of word energies. Well, all words have energy. So do the words that identify the various choices you have in life—even the names of cities, companies, books, universities, and any other object of your consideration. Once you've identified all the options before you, you can use word energy to discover greater insight about each.

Knowing Your Options

When making any decision, it's important to be precise about your options. Clarity is essential with any choice, and that's also true when using word energy to decide. For instance, if you're thinking about moving to England, there would be a great deal of difference between moving to the Isle of Man or to the city of London. Though you may not yet be fully aware of every opportunity, try to use specific words to name each option when doing the methods shown in this chapter. And if you're considering only one option, such as moving to London, don't forget to compare that energy to its alternative, which, of course, would be staying in your original location.

You can use word energy to help you make decisions in any (and every) part of your life—business, personal, financial, or emotional. It can help you choose attorneys, accountants, and other professionals; vacation locations; move options; job choices; and much more. Word energy can also help you choose the best computer, car, furniture, and even the right clothes for meetings and special events. Once you start to really know word energy, you'll be able to discover great insight into all of your options and how they will affect you.

As we look at the various methods available in using word energy for decision making, you may find that you already use some of them to a certain degree. Let's take a look.

Methods in Decision Making with Word Energy

1. Imaging the Visuals That Come with Your Options
2. Sensing Each Option's Impact on Your Energy
3. Tasting the Answer
4. Tapping into the Power of the Written Word

The first step before trying any of these methods is to give each of your options a name. Some will have actual names; other options will just have representing words. Simply determine a word or phrase that indicates each of your various options—the name of a company, a location, a person, or whatever word that would precisely represent each alternative. Even if you're only trying to decide whether or not to take a single course of action, you still need the word or words that reflect that choice.

For instance, if you're wondering whether or not to take a computer class, you could use the words *computer class.* It's best, though, for you to be as precise as possible, such as *computer-programming class, computer-repair class,* or the actual name of the class or its instructor. Of course, as you do any of these methods, do the process with only one option in your mind at a time. Don't let your mind wander or consider an "either-or" scenario or you could get conflicting information. If you do find a number of options popping into your mind, take a deep breath, release them all, and try again.

1. Imaging the Visuals That Come with Your Options

Spontaneous imaging is something you've practiced many times already, just as different images came to mind when you experienced the word *horsepower.* All you have to do is give yourself over to every image and concept that comes to you with each option name. Sometimes you may perceive an image or concept that is absolutely telling as soon as you see it. And sometimes little ideas and images may evolve and tell a story.

Another type of imaging occurs by using image triggers. Image triggers are like word triggers, except that they're visual and conceptual instead of verbal. Both image and word triggers help you tap into your intuition.

You can predetermine to use just about any type of triggering image that works for you. For instance, if you want to know which company would be the best step in your career, you could use an Image Trigger of a boat. In this process, you simply say the name for each option separately. Ask your imaging right brain to give you the idea or picture of a boat with each one. Be spontaneous, and trust the first kind of boat that comes to mind with each option. You may find that one company could be a speedboat, another could be a leaky rowboat without any oars, and one could be a garbage scow—yikes!

You can use just about any type of image as an Image Trigger. I use the boat trigger often. When I do, I focus my attention on the details of the boat that appears—the size, color, condition, movement . . . everything. Other Image Triggers I use are cars, houses, gardens, and roads. But you can use just about anything. If you really like baseball, you can direct yourself to perceive the image of a professional baseball team with each option. If you get the New York Yankees, then you'll know that option could be a winner for you. If you get the name of team at the bottom of the league, then you might want to consider something else. You could also envision a *Monopoly* game board, and spontaneously "see" if you land on Baltic or Park Place with each option.

And how about measuring the options you're considering? If you want to know which job offer might provide the largest opportunity, you can simply ask for the word *inch* or *mile,* and see what you get. I use this process when I want to measure the value in the choices that lie before me—especially when considering investment, real-estate, or financial options.

Big and Little Word Power

Whether you're making an investment, a purchase, or even seeking a new job, you can measure the value of each option before you. Close your eyes and think of the words that represent only one of your options that lie before you. As you hold this option in your thoughts, immediately summon up the image of either an *inch* or a *mile*. Whether you get an image, a sense of size, or simply the word, command yourself to get either an *inch* or *mile*.

Really feel it fully. Let yourself get a clear idea about how
far this choice can take you.

I shared this process with an author friend. She had been struggling with two different, but related, book ideas and wondering
which one to do first. She told me that she didn't really resonate
with the words *inch* and *mile*. That's okay; no word affects everyone in the same way. If there's a word that's not as effective for
you, just find an alternative. That's why it's so important to be on
the lookout for new words. You never know when you're going to
find a word treasure!

I told my author friend not to worry about the words, but
to simply perceive an element of size. Being a visual person, she
perceived images very easily. With one option she got an image
of a big garden with a little part of it missing. With the other
option, she perceived an image of a very small garden, one that
would easily fit the missing part in the other image. Those were
her *mile* and *inch!* She immediately decided to put the two subjects
together, making the second topic just a small portion of a bigger
book focusing on the first.

You can also summon up the idea or image of a path. Look
down the path and see which option will take you the farthest.
Sense or see what the path is like. It may be wide or narrow, rocky
or clear, uphill or straight ahead. All of these images hold messages
for you. No matter what trigger you choose, just be like Einstein.
Trust everything and give your imagination the job, and then
you can see the beam of light that takes you to the right choice.

Determine the names for all of your options. Once you have
the identifying words or phrases in mind, simply do the following
process with each one individually.

Trigger Images for Choice

Close your eyes. Take a deep breath, and bring your
focus inward. Say to yourself the name or word that represents your first option. Make the command, *There's a*

symbol here now. Immediately notice the first image, idea, word, or symbol that spontaneously comes to mind. It may not seem complete, but that's okay. Don't stop or doubt yourself. Just take a moment to let this image or concept play out. Repeat the word that represents this option. Notice everything you perceive and what you feel.

Let that go and now think of the Image Trigger of a boat. What type of boat do you get with this choice? While still holding the word for this option in your mind, notice everything you perceive about this boat, its seaworthiness, and even the water around it.

Take a deep breath and let the boat go. Now imagine a path with this specific outcome. What does the path look like? Where is it going? And how do you feel about taking this path?

Now let all of that go. Take a moment to interpret the meanings of these images. What do they tell you about this option?

Once you're done with this process, be sure to take some notes. Then go back and do the process with each of your other options. During any process, if you start to jump back and forth between options in your mind, take a step away and come back to it later.

The final type of imaging in making decisions is self-imaging. It's easy. All you do is see yourself within the choice you're considering. If you don't tend to be a visual person, you can still do this conceptually. Your right-brain's imaginative process will simply give you concepts and ideas rather than images.

See-for-Yourself Decisions

Close your eyes, and take a deep breath while thinking of a choice you have to make. Simply hold the word or name that represents your first option in your mind. Begin to picture your involvement within it. Indeed, imagine that you've made this decision a long time ago, and you're many months into the outcome.

Use your imagination fully, and really put yourself there. Say the option name again, and be there. Notice how you feel being in that situation, activity, or location. Most important, notice how much enthusiasm you have about living with this outcome for a long time.

Write about your experience after you've finished, and then do the process again with the word that represents each choice individually. When you're done, step away and relax. You don't have to rush your decision. Later you can get a better look at each of your options by using the many other methods of decision making in this chapter.

2. Sensing Each Option's Impact on Your Energy

As you experienced in Chapter 3, sensing the energy of words can take a number of forms, and this is true in making choices, too. Opening yourself to every sense perception fully will give you the insight you seek.

> *"When the ocean surges, don't let me just hear it.*
> *Let it splash inside my chest!"*
>
> — RUMI

Here Rumi gives us a great example of how deeply we can know every experience in life. The most common event can become uncommon—even extraordinary—when we take it inside us and feel the pulse of energy within. When you read Rumi's words, you could sense the splash inside you, too. Your imagination did the work for you automatically. That's what happens when sensing the energy of any word or phrase. And it even happens with words that represent your choices, as long as you open yourself to experiencing their energy in every way. Let them *splash* or *roar* or *beat* inside your chest!

Tuning In to Your Options

Close your eyes and think of the word that identifies a single course of action or an option about which you're deciding. Take a deep breath, and bring that word deep inside you. Notice the energy you sense. How do you feel physically? Do you feel small and compact or large and expansive? Say the word again. Do you feel heavier or lighter? Is there any part of your body that you notice with this word? And if so, what is it, and how does it feel?

Now begin to open yourself to the emotional energy, too. Put that identifying word in your heart, and really feel it emotionally. Do you feel happy or nervous, excited or afraid, sad or hopeful? Notice any and every feeling that enters the heart. Really sense how you feel emotionally with this word for a few minutes.

Now take a moment to feel the action that this word evokes from you. Are you lifted up and inspired, or are you too inert to take any action? Are you excited to go forward, or perhaps, feeling vulnerable—wanting to run the other way? Are you feeling blasé—uninterested in doing anything one way or the other? Notice what type of action the energy of this word elicits from you.

After you've finished this process, sense the energy of the other options. Do the name of each one separately. Be sure to take some notes about your experiences with each in your journal.

3. Tasting the Answer

It may seem weird at first to try to taste the energy of a word. Some people do have a little difficulty with this kind of sensing.

If it's not something you particularly like, you can use any of the other methods. But do give it a try. Remember, you can't have a "wrong" impression. Everybody's experience is going to be different, and yours will be unique to you. You can actually sense the taste of any word. As a matter of fact, it's a good idea to taste your words when you're about to say something about another person. You'll probably find you won't want to swallow bad words—or say them. So, get ready to taste the words representing your options. You may find that some of them may not be as sweet as you thought.

A Matter of Taste

Close your eyes and think of the word that reflects one of your options in a decision you have to make. Imagine yourself putting the word in your mouth and tasting it on your tongue. You won't have an actual taste; you'll simply imagine a taste. Or you may even recall a taste or remember a food. If something doesn't come to you right away, command a taste or a food to come to mind—any taste like sweet, salty, savory, sour, bitter, or maybe even metallic.

Notice the first taste, and also sense any texture or quality. Most important, be aware of how you feel emotionally when you put this word in your mouth. Imagine swallowing it. How would you feel ingesting this choice on a long-term basis? Would you like to spit it out? What is your response to tasting this word?

For many people tasting may be one of the more difficult types of sensing to experience, but some people can do it right away. I once had a client who was having trouble deciding which high school would be best for her son. The two schools being considered were the top private schools in the area. St. Patrick's had long been a family tradition, but her son wanted to go to St. Bart's. I told her to close her eyes and actually become her son in her imagination. Then I had her take each name separately into her mouth and taste it. Judging from the look on her face, St. Patrick's might have been a lemon, but St. Bart's tasted like a cookie! She really was able to get in touch with her son's taste in schools.

It's possible to develop taste imagination with practice. Practicing word taste is really very easy. First begin with the words of things that actually have taste. Imagine yourself tasting the word *apple, steak, pudding, pear,* and the like. Then move on to inanimate objects, such as *penny, straw, shoe,* and *pillow.* After you've practiced with a lot of different types of words, you'll develop a taste for tasting their energy! As a matter of fact, once you're familiar with it, tasting words may be one of the fastest methods in decision making.

When you're finished tasting all your options, be sure to write down everything you experienced and how it made you feel. This is important with any and all of the processes in this book, because writing will then engage the left brain, which will help you remember, analyze, interpret, and understand each one.

4. Tapping Into the Power of the Written Word

There is a way, when you're too emotionally involved, to take your own partiality, fears, and predispositions out of the decision-making process. You can actually experience the energy of the written word *without* looking at it. Really? Yes, words carry energy not only on the page, but also right through the page! To prepare for this process, all you have to do is write down the identifying word for each choice on its own piece of paper. Be sure that all of the papers look identical so that you can't tell them apart. If you're only considering one specific issue, you can take this time to get insight about that and about other questions in your life. Simply write one precise name, word, or phrase that represents each question on its own single paper. Then do the following process.

The Writing's in Your Hand

After you've written the word for each option on its own sheet of paper, fold each paper in half and then half again. Do this so you can't see the word or name written inside. Make sure that each sheet of paper is folded in the exact same manner as all of the others. They all need to remain identical and indistinguishable.

Once all of the papers are folded, place them all in a box or basket and mix them up completely. Then take one piece of paper, still folded, and hold it in your hand. Close your eyes and take a deep breath. Know that you are ready to perceive any subtle nuance that comes to you through this word's energy. Everything you experience and any image or symbol that pops up gives you insight about this unidentified option. Notice the energy you sense, the colors, and ideas. And notice what you feel emotionally. Finally, command the image of a boat or a path, and notice the details you get.

Write down everything you perceive on the outside of the paper, even if the words and images seem disjointed and unclear. When you've finished, put that paper down without opening it. Repeat the process with each individual paper, one at a time. Don't try to guess what's written inside! Allow yourself to completely trust every image and subtle sense you perceive, writing your images, ideas, and energetic reactions on the outside of each paper.

Feeling the words' qualities in this way may be a little more challenging than sensing the energy while knowing the word. But don't forget all of the scientists, inventors, and physicists through history used right-brain imaging when they had no words or answers at all. Also remember Emoto's work. The water crystals he tested certainly had no consciousness of the words, but they were influenced by the words' energy nonetheless.

You can use this process in making any kind of decision—about a car, vacation spot, university, career, relocation option, or anything that comes to mind. Just write the names of each choice on its own paper, fold the papers, and sense each one. Let your images, tastes, and senses flow; and then write all your experiences down on the outside of each sheet of paper. Once you're finished with all of your papers, you can open them up to see the insights you've gained. It will take only a few minutes for each one.

The Bottom Line

Don't forget that word energy is first derived from the word's meaning to you. Some words hold a personal meaning for you, and some don't. Most of the images, sensations, tastes, and perceptions will usually give you very clear insights about your decisions. It doesn't take a lot of interpretation when you experience an image that excites, an energy that lifts, or a taste that's sweet. But there are some energy experiences that may not be as immediately apparent. That's all right; that's why it's so important to do different processes over time and to take notes—so that you can see how you experience the many layers of word energy in your options.

Of course, the bottom line in making any decision is to *make the choice that most honors you.* Usually, the words that represent the most honoring options will carry some type of positive energy, while those that don't will usually have a lack of energy or give you some type of negative experience.

Remember that the choice that honors you the most may not be the easiest. Indeed, it can often be the most challenging, because it is the choice that will require you to grow. There can be some choices that *seem* desirable but would not be best at all. And there could be some choices that seem scary or uncomfortable that would really be the most beneficial. If that's the case, what can be done? When you have conflicting feelings, doubts, desires, and wishes that get in the way and confuse the issue, working with these word energy processes will help.

With more important decisions you'll want to try all of the word methods. If you still find yourself up in the air, take your time. Major life decisions don't—and shouldn't—happen overnight. Do some practical investigation. Meditate on which course of action most honors you. Continue to work with all of your imaging, sensing, and tasting experiences. Seek to discover the energy that all the words and names carry—and the insights they show you. When you add word power to all the other considerations, you *will* discover the best path to take.

Chapter 9

YOUR DECLARATION OF INDEPENDENCE

"The greatest griefs are those we cause ourselves."

— SOPHOCLES

There are times when disappointing events in life can really cause enormous grief. But how much sadder is it when we cause ourselves harm and pain—not just once or twice or even a dozen times, but day after day and year after year? That's what happens when we perpetuate hurtful, self-sabotaging habits, habits that can include unhealthy activities like smoking or even decades of negating self-talk and feelings. Bad habits can come in all different colors and sizes. A lot of people take the term bad habit lightly because they consider it to be something they can easily change when they get around to it.

The word *habit* seems to indicate for many a kind of harmless—and perhaps even mindless—activity. But that perspective can become very dangerous. There are some habits that seem harmless but have severely negative consequences: alcohol, food, and chemical addictions; as well as long-term habits of self-loathing, intolerance, or victimization are just some examples. On a day-to-day basis these habits seem to have no immediate effects, and so the behavior is continued week after week.

Any action that is repeated becomes a habit. And negative habits are the rituals in life that diminish success, power, and joy.

Imagine going to a church where the ceremonies there celebrate failures, and the prayers are utterances of lack and unhappiness. In truth, many people attend this place of worship every day without ever leaving home.

Mental and emotional habits of intolerance—whether of self or others—give birth to a little dark thought here, another hurtful word there, a defeating behavior now, another sabotaging action then. Pretty soon what started as mindless, unimportant moments take darkness into a daily or even hourly event. Brick by brick, years and even decades are spent building cathedrals to judgment and negativity.

But not anymore! You don't have to spend another such year, month, or even moment. Starting with one word, you can dismantle the old rituals and build a new monument—a monument to happiness, power, and compassion.

Give Me Liberty

> *"There is greater magic in the word liberty*
> *than in all other words combined!"*
>
> — C.A. WINDLE

There are still some places where personal liberty is thwarted by government. But in spite of this, much of the world now has a level of freedom unknown before modern times. For most people, the search for freedom has turned inward. And once it's found, like all freedoms, it must be enforced.

It's amazing how much people will clamor, fight, and even die for freedom, yet still keep themselves enslaved. There are Trigger Words that help people stop attachments, but none of them is the word *stop*. What's necessary to end self-enslavement is to enforce *freedom*. You can begin to do that by using *freedom* as a Trigger Word. Take a moment to think about one of your negative habits—whether in thought or action—that has caught you in its snare. Hold this habit in your mind as you do the following process.

Word Power for Freedom

Close your eyes and think about a defeating habit you'd like gone. Consider how it already has diminished your sense of well-being. Be aware of its long-term effect on your happiness and success.

Take a deep breath, and say the word *freedom*. Fill yourself now with the energy of being *free*. Again, say the word *freedom* and bring it inside. Really feel the energy of *freedom*. With this word, you see yourself breaking out of the habit—almost as if you're breaking out of the chains that this history has wrapped around you. With another breath you say *freedom* again, and you feel happy, relieved, and excited to be *free* of this habit and history. Really *free*. From now on, whenever this situation comes up again, you take a deep breath and say *freedom*. You become *free*. You step away and find a new thought and a new action to replace this habit. And happily you say to yourself, *Today is my independence day!*

You can use the word *freedom* whenever an old action or thought—from this pattern or any bad habit—springs up. When you use it, you will take its energy inside you and give yourself freedom from this negativity. And you will take up the mantle of positive thoughts and actions. The Trigger Word *freedom* is your proclamation of liberty. With it, every day can be your independence day. If you'd like to alternate this Trigger Word to keep the novelty high, you can use the word *liberty, released, independence, free,* or the Latin *libertas.* You can also refer to the Trigger Words from Chapter 5, *override* and its alternates, to change old habits to new. Though that has a more technical flavor than the emotional power of *freedom*, it's very effective with all sorts of old programming.

I taught the *freedom* Trigger Word process to a number of different clients who had built their own defeating and enslaving habits. One named Cathy had lost her teenage daughter in a car accident, and within a year, her husband had left her. She was caught in a perpetual downward spiral of grief over her daughter and anger at her husband. Now, this grief and anger were certainly valid and natural for Cathy to feel. Everyone should have absolute permission to feel grief or have hurt feelings and express them during difficult and wounding situations. But it had been six years since her daughter's death and five years since her husband left. And she was still spending most of her time—even while she was at work—submerged in angry, painful thoughts and feelings. She had become immobilized and had stopped pursuing any happy endeavors.

I taught Cathy the Trigger Word, *freedom,* and she began to use it every time she was caught in these horrible thoughts. I also gave her some new statements that were more forward thinking to replace the old ones. After she used the word *freedom,* she would follow it with declarations like, *I find a greater power and purpose today,* or commands such as, *I open myself to new ideas and experiences now.* It was also important for Cathy to find greater purpose and fresh expressions of her creativity, which she did through consciously exploring new interests, meeting new people, and pursuing new activities.

It took Cathy a long time and a great deal of perseverance to break free from years of this negative downward spiral. The Trigger Word *freedom* galvanized her determination to take a new direction in every part of her life and stop living in her painful past.

Cathy's was a severe case because of her enormous loss. But some people experience negative emotional and mental patterns for decades, and others for even most of their lives. Some people can have sabotaging physical habits for decades, as well. I have shared this effective Trigger Word with people working on physical habits, too—quitting smoking, losing weight, and overcoming drug and alcohol addiction. And I even had one client, Ken, who had a sexual addiction. His whole story was complex, and he worked very hard in therapy. Ken used the word *freedom* often, and he eventually triggered a whole new direction and purpose. In time he liberated himself from distraction and destruction, and poured his energy into a new career, a landscape-design business that's very successful.

As someone once said, "The price of freedom is eternal vigilance." And so it was with these people. All of them—even Ken—found the Trigger Word *freedom* to be powerful and effective . . . but only to the degree that they used it. When they used it, they were more likely to take the actions that enforced their freedom. If they only made halfhearted attempts and used the Trigger Word, *freedom,* occasionally, they saw only occasional and impermanent results. But those who used it more often were able to build much greater momentum.

Of course, everybody's human, and everyone's going to slip up now and again. But each step toward *freedom* clears the way for the next step, and the next.

It might seem that people who have the most severe habits would have the most difficulty in taking the steps to break them, but that really isn't the case. Those who were most successful were the ones who simply triggered their new words and actions most frequently. That's really all that's needed to hit a critical mass. Regardless of how severe and long-lasting—or mild and seemingly harmless—any habit is, *freedom* is always possible. As a matter of fact, *freedom* is not only the trigger to your release, but it is the happy outcome as well.

So give yourself the *freedom* you seek. It's the most important and hard-won of all human rights. Don't let yourself be the one who keeps it from you.

Change Please

Another great Trigger Word to help give you freedom from the old, negative habits is the word *change.* I call it an insertion word because I insert it into my day with the many little changes I want to make and recognize.

Big changes only come about from heaping up little changes one after the other after the other. In hexagram 57, The Gentle Penetrating Wind, the I Ching tells us that a gentle influence may be less noticeable than sweeping change, yet it is more lasting and permanent.

When you use the word *change* or *Change now* to alter the course of your frequent thoughts and actions throughout your day, you can heap up dozens of little changes that will make your big changes real in the long run. You can also use the word *change* as a reminder that you are becoming a new you in any and every moment.

Changing Word Power

Close your eyes. No matter what you were doing or thinking a moment ago, declare to yourself, *There's a change now.*

Feel that some good *change* is within you. Don't start analyzing what it might be. Just tap into a sense of newness about you. Declare again, *There's a change now,* and feel a wonderful newness coming to your life.

Every time you say *Change now,* there comes a new thought, new energy, and new opportunities—even a whole new world. Whenever you command *Change now,* you make a shift, you sense this newness, and you can feel excitement stir within you.

Chapter 10

Words and Actions—
a Perfect
Combination

"Do the thing, and you shall have the power."

— Ralph Waldo Emerson

We've seen how specific words can trigger precise action. That is the primary purpose of using Trigger Words. But there are lots of actions that you already take every day. When you add special words to these, you can tap a gold mine that already runs through your life.

There is a Latin saying, *facta non verba,* which means *deeds not words.* It is the foundation for that other old saying, *Actions speak louder than words.* You know how strongly your actions speak for you. They are your declarations to the world. But if your words are declarations and your actions are, too, what can happen when you combine the two?

In many ways, words and actions are combined every day—sometimes in good ways, sometimes in not-so-good ways. In English *actions with words* would simply be called rituals. You may think that you would have to go to a church or synagogue or even a Masonic Temple to find a place of ritual in these modern times, but really all you'd have to do is step into just about any room in your home. Most people aren't aware of how many rituals fill their lives because they think of rituals as being only religious or ceremonial in nature. But that isn't so. *A ritual is any activity that is repeated in a similar way over and over again.*

Indeed, rituals are so ubiquitous, they're not just a part of daily life; they are daily life! The more often an action is replicated, the more force it begins to carry. The more a word is spoken, the more it is made true in the manifest world. Frequency creates frequency, or—to put it another way—greater repetition creates greater vibration and power. And you can use the frequency of your daily tasks to lift your power every day.

Everyday Rituals—a Thousand Points of Power

"There is no such thing in anyone's life as an unimportant day."
— ALEXANDER WOOLLCOTT

There are hundreds of little activities that are done every day or regularly throughout the week that have no extraordinary value of good or bad: washing the dishes, making beds, doing laundry, showering, and on and on and on. Now, certainly any of these could take on a harmful quality if negative thoughts or feelings filled the time spent doing them. And although many people do worry during their daily activities, most spend their moments of mundane tasks thinking about what's on their to-do lists, the calls they have to make, or other such sundries. The moments pass, and these uneventful tasks end up being just that—uneventful. But they can be so very much more.

If your *facta cum verba*—your actions *with* words—have the power to create your reality, imagine the influence when you compound specific words with frequently repeated activities. Bringing together what you say with what you do over and over every day can have an explosive impact on the energy you feel and express.

Since you're going to spend time doing all of life's little tasks anyway, you might as well blend them with the Trigger Words that turn those tasks into moments of power. You can lift each and every action—no matter how small or unimportant—to bring huge benefits to your life. All you have to do is bring the right words to your rituals every day.

Greeting the Day

The first action that you take every day is waking up. Some people like to pop right out of bed as soon as they wake, while others take time to gather their forces. No matter how you wake, you can use Power Words with this morning ritual to help you shine all day long.

A New Morning

When you wake up in the morning, close your eyes for just a moment longer. Take a deep breath and fill yourself with the words *New Day. New Beginnings.* Feel yourself stir with a sense of *new opportunities.* Take another deep breath and say to yourself, *New Day, New Beginnings, New Life!* Your energy is renewed. And, like this new day, you feel like *everything is starting anew!*

Forgiveness as a Ritual

There are some days that anger—little or large—can pop up so many times that it can almost become a ritual itself. You may be angry that a person at work stole an opportunity out of your hands, or you may be perturbed that a friend may be talking about you behind your back, or you may be suffering from long-lingering anger at one of your parents who verbally abused you as a child. Whatever's the case, all that has to happen is for you to see them, see their pictures, or even just think of them to have the anger come up again. And with those easy stimuli, you have ample opportunity throughout your day for anger to color your experience.

Happily, if you have many opportunities to feel anger, you also have many opportunities to forgive! Indeed, you can make forgiveness a ritual whether there's a lot of anger in your life or just a little.

For the most part, forgiveness requires a compassionate understanding of the people who have wounded you—their vulnerability and attachment to their ego's perspective (and, sadly, a detachment from their own inner spirit). Understanding and forgiving are gifts you give to yourself. They create peace in your life and lift you out of victimhood and into your own internal power.

Commanding Forgiveness

Think of someone who has made you angry for some reason. It could be your parents, someone at work, a friend, or anyone. It seems that every single time you run into them, you pass their picture—or whenever you even think of them—you often feel hurt and angry. But from now on you can take a moment to create forgiveness instead.

Whenever you think of these people, you take a deep breath and hold the command, *Forgive* deep in your heart. When they come into your awareness, you fill yourself with *forgiveness, understanding, peace, compassion.* You know that your well-being is not dependent on their actions or their points of view. As you hold *forgive* deep inside you, you seek to know that they, too, have a lack of their own. And, whenever you think of them or see them or their pictures, you *understand* their history and *Forgive.*

This process came about as a matter of necessity. I have a client, Liza, who moved home to take care of her sick mother after her father died. Her father had treated her horribly as a child, calling her "no good" and "useless." It was a history she had thought she'd put behind her.

Her mother's home was filled with pictures of her father taken at various ages. They upset Liza, and her first impulse was to take all of them down and put them away. I told her that hiding his pictures would just help her hide from the issue. I asked her to simply live with them for a few weeks, which she barely did, turning away and hastening down the hall as she passed them. Then I taught her the previous process. I asked her to stop and really look at her dad in the picture, taking the time to imagine him as a child, when he was abandoned by his father and left alone with his alcoholic mother.

This was difficult for her at first, but she was determined. Each day she was able to spend a little more time looking at her father, and seeing him as the wounded boy that grew into a hurtful man. Liza understood that his history was no excuse for his behavior— but it was the reason. In time, she was able to forgive him, and she healed herself, too, because she no longer believed that he hated her. She knew that it was himself and his life that he hated. And she hoped that he would find healing, too.

You can do this *forgiveness* process with anyone, whether those involved are from your history or your present. You never have to live with people who hurt you, and you don't have to live with those old wounds either. Ventilating unexpressed feelings about those people helps. That, along with forgiving and understanding their lack, is your key to peace and freedom from your pain.

Opportunities from Morning to Night

There are countless opportunities to combine Trigger Words with little rituals every single day. Whether you're walking down the hall, cooking, shopping, or driving, try to find each chance where you can bring a Power Word and a little moment together.

There's an old Eastern saying, "Before enlightenment, chop wood, carry water. After enlightenment, chop wood, carry water." Enlightenment is an internal state that lives—indeed, must live—in the little moments of life, because that's where life happens. When you direct mindfulness and the right words to even the most mindless moments, you'll be able to apply an enormous creative force to almost everything.

Here are a few more very quick and easy opportunities to create more power through your mundane daily tasks. You can also create your own. They're lurking around every corner and even at the grocery store.

If you're trying to change a bad eating habit, you can make grocery shopping a powerful ritual that will help you with your shopping, and later with your eating. Give the following grocery-shopping Power Words a try. And then add *walking* to your language—and your life.

Grocery-Shopping Word Power

As you're making your food choices, hold such Trigger Words as *healthy, beneficial, empowering, lean,* and *strengthening* in your mind. Every time you say one of those words while shopping, you buy that type of food, bringing beneficial energy back to you. When you buy *healthy, lean,* and *strengthening* foods, you nourish yourself with those qualities. So repeat these words as you reach for the *strengthening, healthy, lean,* and *empowering* foods.

Walking Word Power

Determine to start using a new power declaration, such as *Walking now!* whenever you get the chance. In an office building, say, *Walking now* in your mind and use the stairs when an elevator is available. In a parking lot, you park at a distance and say, *Walking now!* You say the command *walking now* many times every day. And soon you're walking more outside, inside, and everywhere, getting the activity you want.

Down the Drain

There are lots of little daily rituals that can help with weight loss when Power Words and phrases are engaged—from food prep to dish washing to house cleaning. I remember Laura Silva, an insightful mindfulness teacher, sharing the story of how a student of hers did a simple process that garnered some great results. If you'd like to lose some weight, give it a try.

Word Power in the Shower

Every day, when you take a shower, say the words, *The water is easily washing away any unwanted, excess weight.* Repeat this or just the declaration *unwanted weight rinsing away!* several times throughout each shower without any emotional urgency. Then let it go.

Laura's student did this every time she showered. After a while, she began to lose weight, slowly but steadily. Over time, she lost all of the weight she wanted to lose—without, she said, having changed her diet or exercise habits.

Now, to be perfectly honest, I feel pretty certain that there must have been some subtle changes, both in what she ate and in her activity level. After all, focusing on easy weight loss every morning is bound to have an effect on one's choices throughout the day. But either way, she got the results she wanted!

By creating this process as a ritual—which occurs simply by doing it over and over and over again—your experience of it can become reality. Over time, the idea of unwanted excess weight easily washing away from you begins to carry more power. As it starts to feel more and more like your truth, you will begin to change—sometimes even unconsciously—the patterns and responses that you carry around food. Your eating habits and your activity level will actually try to conform to your new truth, rather than the old. Of course, for the most successful weight loss, emotional, mental, and behavioral eating patterns and exercise practices also need to be addressed in a holistic way. But this little practice can be a virtual shot in the weight-loss arm.

So give it a try. Repeat it, repeat it, and repeat it some more. Pretty soon, you'll be washing away your unwanted excess weight by washing away your old belief system about how hard—or even impossible—losing weight could be.

You could use this declaration for other purposes, too. Every time you shower you can wash away anger, bad habits, old wounds, dark feelings, or past issues. By mixing the power of your new words with the energy of activity, your new belief will become your truth. Soon there will be more than just shampoo and water running down the drain—your old habits will be washed away as well!

Make Your Bed with Words

You can use your daily rituals to focus on lifelong goals, like weight loss, healing relationships, or ending negative patterns. But you can also use even the smallest most mundane daily activities to bring real benefit, too. From the time you wake up to the time you go to bed, you can combine your words with your little actions to impact the very fabric of your experience.

Not everybody has the habit of making the bed. But actually, making your bed is a very good thing for a number of reasons. It keeps your space more orderly for feng shui—energy flow—purposes. It makes you feel more organized and effective, which helps you approach your day with a more successful attitude. And, finally, it's more pleasing to the eye and therefore lifts your spirits. (This is true, also, of doing the dishes, clearing your desk, hanging your clothes, and myriad other organizational tasks.)

Now, of course, you can be very successful and blissfully happy even with an unmade bed. Making your bed and doing the dishes aren't necessary for your success and happiness, but they will all help if you add the right focus and words to them. Imagine the kind of power making your bed can have when you consider that over a lifetime an individual will make the bed over 10,000 times! With that kind of Power, your ritual of making the bed can have an impact deep into the night and for years to come.

When you make your bed every day, you can add just a few Trigger Words and a new intention in order to create a whole new experience of sleep and rest. You can actually *Make your bed in joy, and lie in it!*

Word Power Comforter

When you make your bed in the morning, smooth the covers and say to yourself, *a restful, easy sleep within.* Feel the serenity and ease that these words carry, and declare *recuperative, calming, peaceful rest here.* As you finish making the bed, hold a deep experience of your serene, untroubled heart for a moment. Know that you will carry this peace-filled ease throughout your day and be wrapped in a bed of restful sleep tonight and always.

The task of bed making is possibly one of the shortest of all your daily activities, but 30 to 60 seconds a day can add up to a lot of help in your restful, happy nights. You can use a number of different Trigger Phrases, such as *rest and restore; happy night, joyful day;* or *sleep well, live well.* Or you can make one up for yourself. These words won't only help you have a more pleasant night, but they'll also help you bring a focus on great peace and inner serenity all through your day.

Getting a Real Charge

Remember Masaru Emoto's work with the messages in water? Showing or speaking the words *love* and *gratitude* created beautiful and symmetrical water crystals. If that's the case, could these words have an impact on the water you drink? A lot of people believe so. As a matter of fact, a lot of people write those words—and others like it: *power, joy, strength, courage,* and so forth—on little pieces of paper and tape them to their water containers and dispensers.

Emoto's research shows that exposing drinking water to those words would have an extraordinary effect. And you could write those words on your water bottles, too. But there is more that you can do to bring word power to every glass and bottle of water you drink.

I've been doing this little process of charging water for most of my adult life. It was a longtime practice that was happily validated when Emoto's work was published. It's easy, uplifting, and empowering. It takes way less time than any other task you'll do, and it's something that can be done often throughout the day.

This Trigger Word technique brings together the force of words; the creative power of imaging; the impact of frequent repetition; and, last but not least, the potent energy within you!

Drinking Word Power

The next time you have a glass of water in hand, close your eyes, and take a deep breath. Bring your focus into your heart, and bring into you the word *love.* Begin to feel the power of *love* inside you. It's not just an emotion; it's an energy—a palpable force that's now filling you up as your breath comes and goes with ease.

You are filled and moved by the power of *love, absolute love—tireless, limitless, timeless love.* You take another deep breath and focus on the glass of water in your hand. As you do, you begin to send that energy of love from your heart, through your hand, and into the water in your glass. You imagine this easily. It's almost as if the water is sparkling with *timeless, unlimited, powerful love.*

Your water is now charged and alive with the lightning effervescence of *love*. And when you drink it down, it fills you again with an inner explosion of this radiant power and joy.

Charging your water with vibrant and beautiful energy fills you with that same energy. We see in this process—perhaps more than any other—how very much a word is the very action of itself. You may be the conductor of the charge, but the word itself provides the charging action.

"Words are also actions, and actions are a kind of words."

— RALPH WALDO EMERSON

You can use any Trigger Word to fill your water with its own specific energy. You can charge your water with the action of *strength, power, focus, diligence, attention, passion, joy,* or whatever combination of energies you'd like. I have used a number of different words with this process, but I almost always come back to a combination of the words *love* and *power*.

Try to do it with every glass or bottle of water you drink. It only takes a few seconds to light up your water with power and timeless love. You can do it anytime, anywhere. Nobody around you will know what you're doing, but *you* certainly will—all day long!

Actions That Trigger Words

Trigger Words are meant to stimulate certain actions, thoughts, and attitudes, but there are times when the action comes first, as with many regular activities and daily rituals. When you add words to rituals, the words that follow will then trigger more action and greater attention. It is a compounding of idea, force, and repetition—a blending of the recipe, if you will. And it creates a beneficial cycle of words and deeds that make little moments carry big impact. This repetition of actions and words invokes the energy that builds your higher power and a new truth.

"Words must be supported by one's entire conduct."

— I CHING

If you say positive words in your mundane tasks but don't carry them into your heart and behavior in the rest of your life, the conflicting energy will undermine your efforts. So make a ritual of using Power Words frequently.

The simple guideline is this: *Fill your actions with powerful words, and follow those words with action.* The words of profound meaning that you bring to even the smallest actions will make your life sacred every day.

Part III

POWER WORDS FROM OTHER PLACES AND OTHER TIMES

*"Dipped in the wisdom of our ancestors,
words pluck strings reaching far through time."*

— BLAIN BOVEE

Chapter 11

FOREIGN WORDS
THAT HIT HOME

"A different language is a different vision of life."

— FREDERICO FELLINI

Although words of another language may not be the first that come to mind when we want to ignite new and more purposeful action, there are many that are uniquely qualified to do just that. Throughout this section, you'll find many foreign or ancient words to use as triggers, but it's also great fun to go on a quest of your own.

When you find a unique foreign word that strikes your fancy anywhere in your life—whether reading a novel, traveling, or wherever—seek out its meaning and write it down in your journal. If it's something that moves you, then use it as a trigger to—well—move you!

There may be some foreign words that are second nature to you, whether through your background, your studies, or your travels. But there will also be many that are very strange. When you start using a foreign word that's new to you, it won't carry the full impact of its meaning.

Even if you know the meaning in your native language, it's important to cement that meaning to the new word. When I first start using a different language Trigger Word that's new to me, I usually say both the foreign and English words together. After a while, the meaning and energy are linked from one to the other. When that happens, I find I can use them interchangeably—and still very effectively. Of course, if you'd like, you can use the English version as an alternate. Play with them. You may find the actions they trigger aren't foreign at all.

It Will Go Well

This brings us to one of my absolute favorite Trigger Phrases. *Ça ira* (pronounced "sah eer-AH") is a phrase brought into fashion by Ben Franklin in 1776 while in France. It was his response when he was asked how the revolution in America was going—which really wasn't great at the time.

Although it literally means *it will go* or *that will go,* Ben used it to say, *It will go well.*

The phrase became wildly popular during the French Revolution when it was used as a refrain of "Le Carillon National," the banner song of the revolutionaries. With that song, many took the meaning up a notch to *We will win.* The English translation I use as an alternate—when I use one at all—is Ben's original *It will go well.*

Ça ira are just two little and very easy words. For me, they proclaim my belief in a happy, beneficial outcome—though it may not be the exact outcome I expect or desire. As a matter of fact, declaring that a beneficial outcome actually *will* happen means that it doesn't have to happen in only one way. *It will go well* is not synonymous to *It will go the way I want. After all,* going well can go in so many unknown yet positive ways!

Having an attitude of things going well not only helps lift your enthusiasm and optimism, but it also opens you to all sorts of beneficial possibilities other than the one you planned. I use this triggering declaration any time I find myself worried about how a situation is evolving—or concerned about how a project will turn out. It immediately triggers a sense of surety that all really will go well.

Word Power from Ben Franklin

Think of a situation in your life for which you have a hopeful plan. There may be some challenges at the moment, or even to come, and you might find yourself occasionally worrying.

Close your eyes and see yourself there. Take a deep breath, and say to yourself, *Ça ira, It will go well*. And center yourself in that truth. Say again, *It will go well, Ça ira*. And let yourself really feel the certainty of it. Know *it will go well*, and let your worries fall away.

I use this declaration in English and French when referring to little projects and major goals. There isn't a situation that can't be helped by declaring *It will go well*. And judging from the outcome of the American Revolution Ben was describing, *It will go well* may be both a declaration and a prophecy all rolled into one!

What a Wonderful Year!

Holding a surety that a certain situation will go well can truly relieve you of all of your worries about that particular endeavor. Wouldn't it also be great to hold the certainty that things will go wonderfully all year long? Well, there is a Latin declaration that can help you do just that: *Annus mirabilis* ("AN-nus mee-RAH-bil-is").

It means *wonderful year* or *remarkable year*. Even though this term is predominantly used to refer to past years when extraordinary events occurred, I like to use it to trigger my excitement about how wonderful this year is now—and is going to continue to be!

Wonderful Word Power

Close your eyes and take a deep breath. Let go of whatever you're thinking, and simply open your mind and heart.

Say to yourself, *wonderful year, annus mirabilis.* And hold in your heart the excitement of *a remarkable year.* It is so; you can make it so. Say to yourself again, *annus mirabilis, remarkable year!* And take a moment to breathe in the wonder!

Some people may think that calling a year wonderful won't make it so, but they'd be surprised. And so will you! Though you won't say *remarkable year* just to convince yourself, you will be convinced because it will trigger thoughts of all the remarkable things this year holds. And the smile that comes to your face will be *mirabilis!*

In Courage

"Courage is not the towering oak that sees storms come and go; it is the fragile blossom that opens in the snow."

— A L I C E M . S W A I M

The word *courage* comes from the Middle English and Old French word *corage,* which meant *heart* or *spirit.* This seems like the perfect meaning to me because courage is a gentle strength that perseveres and pushes through—a strength that comes from the heart and the spirit within.

There are times when you may feel too uncertain about starting something new, too timid to reach out to someone, or maybe you're a little too frightened to pursue something risky. Whatever the situation, what's needed is *courage,* the strength and fortitude to push through—deal with what's challenging you, instead of holding back and withdrawing.

Whenever I find myself in such a situation, I use the original, *corage* (pronounced "Kor-ahj"), because it reminds me that boundless courage comes from the spirit within. The original Middle English form is unique, which keeps the energy higher than the more common *courage.* Give both a try, and see which one works for you.

Courageous Word Power

Close your eyes, and imagine yourself in one of those moments when you're feeling reserved, timid, or hesitant. Bring it to mind, and notice how you feel.

Now, take a deep breath and say to yourself, *Corage.* Bring your focus inside to the deepest part of your heart. Say *Corage* again, and declare *I am filled with the strength, power, and courage of my spirit.*

You feel a stirring of initiative, confidence, and purpose within. The great force of *courage* seems to grow with every breath. Every time you say *Corage* it incites you to act and makes you ready to go in any direction you want. You are more than inspired; you are emboldened!

I have a client named Graham who had a management position in a sizeable international company. Though he was a very confident man, he did have some trouble when dealing with two members of the executive management staff. Actually, everyone had a problem with those two. They were short-tempered and critical of most people who worked for them. Graham began to use the Trigger Word *Corage* to tap into his inner strength before every meeting with these two executives. Not only was he calmer and less ruffled by these meetings, he eventually also got to the point where the behavior of these men never bothered him again. From that time forward he experienced a gentle, unflappable courage at meetings and throughout his day.

And If You Fall . . .

Of course, even during the most remarkable year, there are going to be some setbacks and defeats. There's a world of difference between the word *defeat* and the word *defeated.* One describes an event; the other describes a state of mind. It's possible to suffer a hundred defeats and never be defeated.

This is especially true if you know that defeat is a way to victory. Such was the attitude of the tireless experimenter Thomas Edison, the Wizard of Menlo Park in 1879. He and his team tried hundreds and hundreds of different filaments before finding the right one for his incandescent lightbulb. Those that failed weren't considered defeats. They were just steps on the way to victory (and sometimes steps on the way to other discoveries).

You can see your life as a great experiment, and you never have to feel defeated. The opportunities that don't work only help you find your way to those that do.

> *"This thing we call 'failure' is not the falling down,*
> *but the staying down."*
>
> — MARY PICKFORD

Falling down is an inevitable part of life. Instead of feeling defeated, a fall can actually move you to try again—more excited than ever that you are even closer to your goal.

There's a wonderful Latin Trigger Word that I use in such times, often combining it with its English counterpart, which I also really like. It's *resurgam* ("reh-SUR-gahm"). And it means *I shall rise again*.

Word Power on the Rise

Close your eyes and recall a time when you experienced a defeat of some sort. No matter how you felt then or may still feel, you now know it was not the end, but a step along the way.

Take a deep breath and say to yourself, *Resurgam! I shall rise again!* And with that you begin to see the next step before you. You have a new sense of intention, a new hope. You say again, *Resurgam, I shall rise again!* And with another deep breath, you feel your energy, your power, and your purpose rising.

I love this very potent proclamation. Harry Potter could have used this a number of times in his dealings with Voldemort! It always seems to impart an immediate sense of power and new beginnings. And you don't only have to use it with a defeat. Try it anytime you're feeling down or low in energy, and you won't stay down for long.

A Powerful Idea

Just like words, ideas have a substantial creative force. Creativity takes lots of forms—writing a poem, drafting a contract, designing a room, laying out a marketing campaign, forming a partnership or a business proposal, composing a song, solving any kind of problem, and just about every task—large or small—that requires thought and resourcefulness. Most people think that finding life's little solutions is just busy work, but when you put your imagination into it, it's creative. Whether you're building a house or building a theory, your imaging is key to any creative endeavor.

"A rock pile ceases to be a rock pile the moment a single man contemplates . . . within him the image of a cathedral."

— Antoine de Saint-Exupéry

Here's a little process you can use to engage the imaginative right brain in any of your creative pursuits. The Trigger Word is a simple one: *Powerful Idea.* I often use it with the French: *Idée-force* (pronounced "ee-DAY forse"). I would recommend that you use both until the French is strongly anchored in its meaning for you.

Creative Word Power

Think of any creative project that's been a focus of your hopes or attention lately. Close your eyes and feel the energy as you say to yourself *idée-force,* a *powerful idea.* As soon as you think these words, you open yourself completely, and an image comes to mind. It's an immediate response—you make yourself perceive an image or an idea without hesitation. What is the first thing you get?

Whenever you say the words *powerful idea* or *idée-force,* you immediately ask yourself, *What is the first symbol, image, or thing I see?* Even if what you perceive seems simple or even silly, it represents the next step in your creative process. It's another piece in your creative puzzle, and it's the beginning of a *powerful idea.*

As with any foreign language, *idée-force* might not have as much energy as the English version for you at first. If so, just use the words *powerful idea.* Or you can choose another word that triggers your imaginative response. As you work with Trigger Words, you'll find some of your own that can ignite very powerful ideas. I love the previous quote so much that I like to use its imagery and use the cathedral as an analogy for my creative project. I say to myself, *idée-force! What is the rock pile for this cathedral?*

Be open to the foreign words. They often carry a more mystical power with them. Whichever word you use, however, be sure to take immediate action by focusing on the first image, symbol, or word that comes to mind. Make yourself get a response from your right brain. Trust it without doubt or hesitation. The creative force of your life lies within your imagination—as does your intuition. Use the power of words to help them grow.

This symbol process is very similar to the Image Trigger method in Chapter 8. You can simply open yourself to perceiving the first symbol or image you get, or you can predetermine the type of symbol you want to use and then see how it presents itself to you.

I taught this Trigger Word to Elaine, a client who works in the fashion industry in Paris, and now she uses it during many of her design processes. If she's unsure by what fabric to use with a certain design, she will say *idée-force* and make herself immediately imagine bolts of fabric. Then she would notice which would be the most prominent in her mind.

Other times, Elaine simply opens herself to the first thing that springs to mind. In one instance when she was dissatisfied with a sleeve design that she was working and reworking, she closed her eyes and said, *Idée-force*. Immediately, she got the idea of half a baseball cap. She decided to try a greatly altered cap sleeve, and, though it took some time to evolve, in the end she was quite pleased with it. She said it was one of the most unique sleeves she had ever done.

If an image or symbol doesn't come your way when you first start doing this process, be sure to keep practicing. This is true with your use of all Power Words. You can go to the hardware store and buy every tool available, but they won't build anything if you don't use them. Anything worth achieving is worth practicing. So train yourself. Make it a habit, and plant it in your daily behavior. Invoking a *powerful idea*—in creative endeavors and in the little moments of everyday life—can be a really powerful idea!

Chapter 12

THE POWER OF PRAYER

*"To pray is to expose the shores of the mind
to the incoming tide of God."*

— RALPH W. SOCKMAN

D o you ever invoke the assistance—or even the presence—of
an unseen force? Do you send up a prayer when you get in
a bind? Perhaps you may do one or the other—or maybe feel you
do none at all. But actually you probably use various forms of
invocation and prayer every day.

Many people see prayer as an outdated ceremony belonging to
older times and more primitive minds, yet there have always been
powerful benefits to prayer. In a study led by Dr. Mitch Krucoff
at the Duke Clinical Research Institute, five groups of patients
were given the same traditional—and excellent—medical care that
Duke provides. But remote prayer was said for only one group. This
group had a 50 percent higher recovery rate than the control group
and a significantly higher rate than all of the other groups being
studied. (We'll see more about this and other healing studies in
Chapter 14: "Healing Prayers.")

Prayer and invocation can be powerful tools in life—not only
in healing, but also in work, relationships, family, and practically
any possible endeavor. I remember the story of a man named Amos
Jacobs who pounded the pavement for months and months and
even more months trying to develop a new career direction for
himself. Day after day opportunities were lost, and doors were

slammed in his face. Finally, discouraged and despairing, Amos went into a church and said a few prayers. Within 24 hours he had two jobs.

This is the story of the actor Danny Thomas, who went on to become one of early television's greatest stars. He was a writer, movie actor, and club performer, who also created his own production company—one of television's busiest at its time.

That day in church, Danny had prayed to St. Jude, the patron of lost causes. In profound gratitude, Danny founded St. Jude's Children's Hospital, which treats all children who come, without requiring their family to pay. It is one of the world's prominent hospitals in the treatment of childhood cancers.

Although Danny was a spiritually devout man, he was just another guy looking to move from obscurity to acting success. We are all—in our own sense—that guy, looking for ways to reinvent ourselves and reach our dreams. Prayer, in all of its variations, is one of those ways. And it's a way that belongs to everyone. You don't have to be a monk, a nun, a priest, or even religious at all in order to successfully use invocation and prayer. All you have to do is pray!

Types of Prayer

There is a very slight distinction between invocation and prayer. Not all invocations are prayers, but many prayers are invocations because they often call upon God, some divine force, deity, saint, or spirit. (We'll take a deeper look at invocations in the next chapter.)

Prayers can take many different forms—praise, blessing, petition, confession, thanksgiving, intercession, adoration, or even simply a spiritual conversation with God. Sadly, for too many, prayer only comes when it's time to ask for something.

"God and the doctor we alike adore,
But only when in danger, not before."

— JOHN OWEN

As John Owen tells us, a lot of people don't call God—or the doctor—until they're in trouble. And so it is with prayer. Asking and pleading is what prayer means to many. Indeed, the synonyms for *pray* in most dictionaries include *appeal, plea, entreaty, beseech, supplicate, implore,* and even *beg.*

The word *prayer* originates from the Latin *precari.* This is also the root word for the English *precarious* (originally meaning *dependent upon the favor of another person*). Now *precarious* means *uncertain, risky,* and *insecure.* Anyone would feel this way relying on another's favor! And a lot of people pray because they feel insecure.

Prayer in a Panic

Please understand, it's not a bad thing to ask the powers that be and the world of energy for help, healing, guidance, and support. But once asked, belief and trust are imperative.

> *"Whatever you ask for in prayer,*
> *believe that you shall receive,*
> *and it shall come for you."*
>
> — MARK 11:24

Trust is sadly lacking when one prays with urgency. As a matter of fact, in any situation of need or want, urgency can actually undermine the outcome. Urgency sends the message that you're uncertain the outcome you seek will happen. *Urgency, at its highest pitch, is fear.*

Prayer Works in the State of Trust

> *"Faith is the substance of things hoped for,*
> *the evidence of things not seen."*
>
> — HEBREWS 11:1

A sense of urgency—in life and in prayer—carries with it an undercurrent of uncertainty and lack. To be full, you must see yourself as full. To be strong, you must sense yourself as strong. Of course, if you are praying for help to get a job or praying for healing of a serious illness, there could be a lot of uncertainty and even fear. These are valid feelings, and you shouldn't make yourself wrong for having them. But try to let go of the fear and urgency, and fill your heart with belief and trust.

As you pray, envision the most joyful outcome. See all the forces in the world rallying to bring this goal to fruition. Trust it and know that it is so. And if you have trouble believing at first, remember, "Act as if ye have faith, and faith shall be given ye." With repeated effort, the words you speak will become real.

I have a client, Peggy, who had had two miscarriages and was trying to get pregnant again. Besides doing what her doctor told her, she was urgently reciting different prayers many times a day. And whenever she became even more frightened that she wouldn't conceive, she would triple and quadruple her efforts. She was filling her days and her life with anxiety.

That energy had to change, so I taught her some Trigger Words that could help her let go of her attachment to outcomes. I suggested that besides praying for a baby to also pray for inner peace and trust. I recommended the following simple, little prayer by Robert Louis Stevenson.

Prayer for Courage and Happiness

*"O God grant me courage, gaiety of spirit
and tranquility of mind."*

With effort and focus, Peggy was able to let go of her urgency. After some months, she was also able to conceive. With her prayers and her doctor's help, she had a healthy and happy little boy.

When you have a situation that makes you afraid or urgent, you can say this prayer or make one up for yourself. Change the words around or add new words like *happiness, peace, trust,* or *faith* to make this prayer your own. Then, once your prayers are said, let them all go. Rest in the peace of knowing that which you seek—or something better— shall be realized.

Live Your Prayers

If prayers, Trigger Words, invocations, and Power Words are going to make an impact in your life, you have to *use* them in your *daily* life. To do that more easily, write your favorite ones on index cards, put them where you will see them, and take them with you when you're on the go. Even with Power Words and prayers, your success is relative to your effort and your trust. Making a regular effort will bring a bigger payoff.

Prayers combine your energy and theirs to bring assistance, but they are not necessarily magical, quick fixes. Your prayers are the words that go forth into the world, attracting and creating the highest outcome. Yet, while prayers are made of words, they can often have a greater energy than your other words. Since prayers are usually said with greater reverence, devotion, purity, and purpose, the words said in prayer tend to be more rarified and sacred.

Of course, no matter how holy your words of prayer are, in order to support their success, you must hold them in your life. Prayer sanctifies the moment, but you can make holy all the moments of your life. You must *live* your prayers. Your behavior and attitude needs to reflect your prayers. If you pray for love, fill yourself with love. If you pray for abundance, fill your life with value. In this way you don't just pray with words; you pray with your actions. You pray with your life. And when you do that, the prayers you say will shift from entreaty to reality and then to thanksgiving.

Loving Prayer

Although the following prayer could be considered an invocation because it calls on angelic assistance, it is also a declaration and prayer sending forth the intention for love.

Prayer for Love

Oh, Archangel Raphael,
who brought Sarah and Tobias together in joy,
bring to me one who is loving and giving.
I will do my part by being loving and giving to myself—
in every thought, word, and deed.
I shall open my heart to your guidance
and fill my life with love.

The Archangel Raphael is the patron angel of love as well as healing and travel. You can also pray to the other Archangels—Michael for courage, strength, and power; Uriel for initiative, transformation, and creativity; and Gabriel for better communication with loved ones and for any project or career in communication, from marketing to writing a book. We will see more of Raphael in Chapter 14, "Healing Prayers," and more about finding love in Chapter 19.

Give Thanks

"It is a rude imposition to come to God
asking for anything without saying thanks for past blessings."

— LEHMAN STRAUSS

Prayers of thanksgiving may be the most important prayers of all. When you take the time to be aware of all that makes you grateful, it's easy to remember your happiness. It's really not necessary to list all of your many gifts, but when you give thanks daily, it gives you an ongoing positive look at your life.

The Energy of Thanksgiving

Close your eyes and take a relaxing breath. Bring a deep sense of *gratitude* inside you. Fill yourself with peace and a profound sense of happiness—not just for all you have, but for all you are—the indwelling self whose power, purpose, and brilliance knows no bounds. Take another deep breath and be *grateful,* now, in every breath and every cell. Gently say *thank you.*

You Can Pray for Anything!

> *"O Lord, send me a good tenor—cheap."*
>
> — LILIAN BAYLIS

Lilian Baylis was a theater, ballet, and opera-house manager in London in the late 1800s and early 1900s. One of her theaters, perhaps one of the most famous in the world, was the Old Vic. Like many theatrical ventures, the Old Vic was beset with financial problems.

Much to the dismay of her company, it was a common habit, whether in her office or the theater (though happily, not during a play) for Miss Baylis to actually fall to her knees in supplication asking God to send her any number of cheap—but good—actors, tenors, dancers, and sopranos. Lilian continued praying and receiving through her money troubles, and the intervention must have succeeded. The Old Vic is with us still, just a few steps from Waterloo station. But you've got to get your tickets in advance!

Though you can pray for anything, you must never pray that harm comes to another—not even to those who have hurt you. If there is someone who has harmed you or others, you may want to pray about the situation. There are two different prayers you can make at these times. You can pray for the safety and happiness of those being wounded. And, in order to support that happening, you can also pray for wisdom and compassion to fill the hearts and minds of those responsible. As a matter of fact, praying for compassion for everyone is a pretty good idea.

Prayers of Compassion and Well-Being

The following two prayers can be called blessings, of a sort. Even though these came to me through the American Buddhist author Jack Kornfield, they have long been used by many people around the world who embrace the principles of compassion and loving-kindness. I open or close my meditations with these almost daily.

Prayer of Loving-Kindness and Wellness

May I be filled with loving-kindness.
May I be well in body and mind.
May I be safe from inner and outer danger.
May I be truly happy—and free.

Prayer for Increased Happiness

May you be joyful.
May your happiness increase.
May you not be separated from great happiness.
May your good fortune
And the causes for your joy and happiness
continue to grow.

You can change these lines from a blessing to a declaration by changing the verb, for instance, *I am filled with loving-kindness.* You can also extend these blessings to yourself and many more people by using any appropriate pronoun such as *I, you, he, she, they,* and *all.* Close your eyes and hold that person or group in your mind when you say these prayers.

What Are You Praying to Change?

"It is strange that in our praying we seldom ask for a change of character, but always a change in circumstances."

— ANONYMOUS

Whatever we can make better in our exterior life is nothing to the improvements that can happen within. You can use each prayer request for something in your outer world to trigger inner actions. If you're praying for love, love yourself and create a generous heart. If you're praying for success, act with confidence and see yourself as worthy. *Whatever you seek to gain, seek to live and also to give.*

Here are two prayers that bring the gaining and giving together. The first reminds us that outer success is linked to inner good. It was written by Rabbi Lionel Blue in the first person plural, but I've changed it to the singular for your use.

Prayer with No Limits

There is no limit to my ascent,
for there is no limit to the good I can do.
There is no joy I cannot have,
there is no end to giving.

Prayer in Service to Others
(From Mother Teresa of Calcutta)

Make us worthy Lord,
To serve our fellow human beings
Throughout the world
Who live and die in poverty and hunger . . .
And by our understanding love,
Give peace and joy. Amen.

Making Peace

Imagine what the world could be if everyone would pray for peace every single day! Having that many people feeling and expressing the word *peace* and its energy would make a huge difference. And with their prayers for peace, all those people would be more determined to make peace in their own hearts and in their own lives.

> *"Peace in the world relies on individuals finding inner peace."*
> — THE DALAI LAMA

I pray for peace frequently and hold the quality and energy of *peace* in my meditations. The following is a little, easy prayer that I say any time throughout my day when the idea of peace springs to mind. You can use this prayer when you get angry or when you want to bring peace to yourself and to the world. It's a favorite of mine and also of the schoolchildren in Northern Ireland.

Prayer for Peace Everywhere

Peace in the city,
Peace in the house,
Peace in my heart,
And peace everywhere.

If you'd like, you can do as I sometimes do and simply use the last two lines: *Peace in my heart; peace everywhere.* Say those declarations as frequently as you can remember. And whenever you do, take a moment to turn your mind inward. Feel yourself fill with peace, and imagine peace filling the hearts of everyone and wrapping around the world.

Prayer, Poetry, and Meditation

As important as prayer is to a life of creation and discovery, it's only one part of the formula. You've already seen the contribution your words and actions can make, but there is one action that cannot be equaled by any other. That's meditating.

In a small way, the little word exercises you've been doing throughout this book are mini-meditations, because they are an internal experience. Meditation requires you to go within—not just mentally, but in every inner sense.

Many people have said that prayer is a conversation with God, but conversations aren't only one-sided; they require listening and feeling, too. To make a prayer a meditation, it must be brought within. It must be known and felt deeply, as a stirring energy inside. You can take any prayer—just as you can take any word—and hold it, not just as an idea, but as a profound experience. You can also make poetry into a prayer or a meditation. The following is a meditation that has been adapted from William Blake's poem *Auguries of Innocence*. The only change that I made was to add the pronoun *I*.

Meditation—Eternity in an Hour

I see a World in a Grain of Sand,
And a Heaven in a Wild Flower,
I Hold Infinity in the palm of my hand,
And Eternity in an hour.

Take a deep, relaxing breath and slowly read this poem again. Consider for a moment that heaven flowers here on earth in everything of beauty.

Imagine, now, that you're holding infinity in the palm of your hand. Bring that feeling inside you, and put yourself in the experience of it fully.

Take another deep breath, and sense it. See it.

Think now, that all eternity is contained in the next hour. Hold that in your heart. What do you feel?

All of these prayers can open the door to a higher life, but there are so many more prayers yet to find. So be sure to take your quest further on your own. There is great poetry in the world, too. Each and every verse can become a sacred prayer when you hold its truth in your heart.

You can make a prayer in any moment of your life. You could pour a glass of orange juice and feel thanksgiving for how it nourishes you. You could look at your child or parent and recognize a divine light inside. You could send a blessing to the slow driver in front of you who tries your patience. Most of all, know that any moment in which you hold love is a prayer. As Theresa of Avila said,

"Prayer doesn't consist of thinking a great deal,
but of loving a great deal."

If you live your life in the same way you pray—from a place of humility, inner quiet, and a sense of the sacred, you really will see heaven in every flower and hold eternity in your hand.

Chapter 13

Invocation—Sending Trigger Words Forth

*"Eat and carouse with Bacchus, or munch dry bread with Jesus.
But don't sit down without one of the gods."*

— D. H. Lawrence

L ike a good part of the language we use, the word *invoke* comes
from the Latin. It is the root word *invocare,* which means *to
call* or *to call on.* Many of the prayers from the previous chapter
and, indeed, most prayers in general are invocations because they
usually make a call to some higher being or to a force beyond.

Probably, the one most often called in any invocation or prayer
would be God. In times gone by, the Muses would be invoked to
help assist the creative process. And those in ancient Greece or
Rome would have called upon their many deities for help with
everything from bountiful crops and fertility to healing wounds
and successful battles. Today people use invocation to call the
Divine, the angels, saints, their higher guides, and even their loved
ones who have passed into spirit.

What a lot of people don't realize is that it's also possible
to invoke energies and qualities. When we say words, we invoke
the energy of those words. The energies of nature—such as the
elements—can also be invoked. The Native American Indians,
Chinese, and many older civilizations know this. Yet, of all
that might be invoked, perhaps the one that is neglected most

but should be on top of the list is one's own inner being, one's own spirit.

No matter whom or what you call, the invocation is not only an invitation, but it is also catalyst for energy and action. You can invite even more action by frequently using invocation—as well as Power Words and prayer—on a repeated basis. Be sure to put your favorites on index cards as a reference to use throughout your day. Now, let's take a look at all that invocation does.

Invocation: Reasons and Results

There are many valuable reasons to call for help in this hectic and complicated world. No matter what we could do on our own, we can do it more easily when we combine our energies with others. Invocation helps us make that call—to others and to the forces that support us. Let's look at the important reasons to engage in invocation and then explore each item individually.

Invocation Motivation

1. Invocation is a form of powerful Trigger Words sparking responses from others.

2. Invocation verbalizes your intention and creates a call to action.

3. Invocation helps you stay alert to opportunity.

4. Invocation deepens your relationship with helpers and with the creative forces in the world.

5. Invocation significantly increases your power for manifestation and success.

1. Invocation as a Powerful Trigger

All Trigger Words are invocations because they solicit energy. But invocations themselves stimulate the most action because they summon others to join forces with you. Energy joined is energy accelerated! Be aware, however, of one pitfall that can come when making a call to others—that is the belief that you don't have to take any action for yourself.

Imagine that you have a very large task to do, for instance, painting the interior of your house. You could call a large group of friends who are happy to help. But how long would they make an effort if they saw you doing nothing yourself? Not very long. The effort you make toward your intention combines with the unified forces to achieve success. It is invocation redoubled.

2. Invoking Your Intention for Action

When assistance with something specific is desired, a simple call becomes a call for action. Invocation sharpens your focus on a precise intention and vocalizes it. Once vocalized, the steps required to take action can become clearer and more exact. For example, instead of invoking help from above to lose weight, ask for help in making healthier choices in exercise and at mealtime. This intention puts the action in your hands and creates momentum. Then, when you take that action, it accelerates the energy. Soon it all snowballs together, gaining size and speed in the direction of the goal you seek.

3. Alert to Opportunity

When you've made a focused and pure statement of intention through invocation, you become more open to receiving and more alert to the opportunities that await you. Here's an invocation that you can use for just about any purpose.

Invocation—Open to Receive

I open myself to receive and create [name of intention here].
I will stay alert to every opportunity,
and I will do my part.

With this invocation, you can choose whom or what you want to call, from God, to your higher self, to—quite literally—the powers that be. You can pray for others or choose your own intention if you prefer. Fill in the blank with what you're seeking to receive or create. As long as you do your part, whatever you desire is available to you, including courage and strength; a loving relationship; a new home; a peaceful heart; greater discipline; a promising career; and assistance with a problem, a project, a quest—anything.

4. Deepening Your Relationships

If you believe in the world of energy, you very likely believe in a spiritual reality that exists beyond the physical. This affords you a wealth of assistance—and assist*ants*—that the practice of invocation can help you joyfully develop. Even if you only call your higher self and the God of your understanding, those relationships are well worth deepening. Of course, you can also enhance your personal relationships when you open your heart to love and invoke loving treatment. (You can find more about invoking love in Chapter 19.) And finally, you can also solicit the forces that abound in the world of energy and nature.

5. Manifesting Success

When you invoke the muses, those in spirit, God, your higher self, or the energies in the universe, you increase the "lift" in your project or intention. With invocation many forces come together, including your own will and Universal momentum. The energy becomes so high and so focused that the outcome becomes much more attainable. The attracting forces are connected by intention. Invoking your higher self enlists a broader vision, a greater strength, and a higher level of energy that connects you with untold helpers. Together, your collective ability for manifesting your goals becomes absolutely irresistible.

Invoking Nature's Energies—Lightning in a Bottle!

Invocation is expansive. You don't have to only call upon angels, saints, or other individuals to use it. You can also call the natural forces of the universe around you—forces that are far more available than you think and that carry an energy all their own.

The following invocations are designed to call upon wonderful and unlimited natural powers. They're simple, yet profound. They come from the Native Americans who have always had an abiding relationship with the natural world and have relied upon the forces that thrive within it.

If you'd like to do a visualization with these words, simply imagine their energies moving through you and around you. For earth, feel nurtured, supported, and grounded. For the moon, sense the reflective, quiescent peace within. For the sky, feel yourself expanding and going outward. And finally, for the sun, let yourself fill with creative light, and then feel it shining forth.

19th-Century Navaho Invocation

I ask all blessings.
I ask them with reverence,
Of my mother the earth,
Of the moon, the sky, and sun my father.

The version shown below is a shorter option, if you prefer. It may be faster to say, so you can tap into these elements any time. Their great power is always there for you. Such is the nature of nature!

With reverence I ask all blessings,
Of the earth, and moon, of the sky, and sun.

Here is an Apache invocation that is similar to the Navaho but is somewhat more lyrical. The Navaho invocation acts more like a trigger. You can use it to immediately call and focus those energies. The Apache invocation below is a little more like a poem or a blessing. Remember, with this and with any prayer, invocation, or trigger, you can change the pronouns to *I* or *me,* to *they* or *them,* to *she* or *he,* to *all* or *we.* As a matter of fact, I would recommend that you say the following (and the Buddhist prayers in the last chapter) using various pronouns as you think of different people, families, and groups. It will widen your perspective and send the blessings of nature abroad in the world.

Apache Invocation and Blessing

May the sun bring you new energy every day.
May the moon softly restore you by night.
May the rain wash away your worries.
May the breeze blow new strength into your being.
May you walk gently through the world and know its beauty
all the days of your life.

It only takes a few moments to take a deep breath and speak the gentle words from these invocations, but when you do, your spoken and heartfelt energy achieves four important things:

- First, it connects with the flow and synchronicity of the universal rhythms of life;

- Second, it causes you to pause and reflect on the natural resources around you and within you, shifting your consciousness immediately, and focusing your intention to tap into them.

- Third, it puts forth your request for assistance, sending your desires to the world of energy and invoking the forces that are waiting for your call.

- Finally, it focuses your own energies and intentions, directing your action toward the desired results.

Triggering Blessings

"Use this word without a flip or degrading tone, naturally, and you will see that the word <u>Blessings</u> has Blessings of its own. All you have to do is use it to feel Blessed."

— KENTON KNEPPER

Legend has it that during the plague, Gregory the Great would say *God bless you* to people who sneezed because sneezing was an early symptom of the disease. He was not only wishing well to those people; he was also asking God to keep the plague away from them.

The word *blessings* is very powerful and conveys much more than just your good wishes to others. If you look into all of the meanings of this very dynamic word, you'll find that when you bless people, you're also praising them, expressing gratitude to them, asking for divine favor for them, and, perhaps most important, declaring them hallowed or sacred. The words *God bless you* or *Blessings* also help to trigger a remembrance of the rarified power within—lifting the experience for all concerned to a measureless sense of Divine self.

So begin to use this word more frequently in your life—both in your writing and your speech. Whether signing a letter or an e-mail, *Bless you* or *Blessings* is a good intention. It can refer to the person to whom you're speaking as well as to yourself—or even to others. Do the following process to align yourself to this very dynamic word and invoke the blessings of the world.

Word Power Invoking Blessings

Close your eyes and take a deep, relaxing breath. Begin to hold the word *blessings* in your heart. Feel yourself fill with *blessings* in every cell and every breath— blessings of power, blessings of love, blessings of a life of joy. Feel these blessings permeate your energy.

Take another deep breath, and say *blessings* again. Recognize that all who are blessed are filled with a sacred power and peace. And every time you say *blessings*, you fill the moment and yourself with an incandescent warmth and the light of eternal *blessings*.

It's helpful to repeat this process occasionally in order to continue your connection with this profound energy. To keep your level of interest high you can use variations, even another language. (See Appendix 3 for other alternatives and foreign translations of *God bless you*.) Remember to repeat the process using both the old and new words, filling the new with the energy of the original.

A friend of mine named Betsy combined this word with the word *bliss* to create her own Power Word, *blissings*, wishing *blessings* for a *blissful* day. She used *blissings* to sign all her e-mails, and since her job required a lot of that, she soon found herself feeling happier—more *blissful*—on a regular basis. The people she wrote were quick to let her know how pleased they were to receive that intention. She had brought them and herself *blessings of bliss*.

Regardless of which form of *blessing* you share with others, be sure to take a moment to feel that energy and quality for yourself *every time* you use that word. You don't have to do the whole process. Just recall and sense in that moment, the energy of glorious *blessings* for all involved—and for everyone everywhere. (In Chapter 16, we'll take a look at using this Trigger Word to turn dark situations to light.)

Your Legions of Helpers

*"If you are seeking creative ideas, go out walking.
Angels whisper to a man when he goes for a walk."*

— RAYMOND INMON

If we take a look at Charles Dickens's life, we'll see that Inmon wasn't exaggerating. When in the throes of writing his wonderful story *A Christmas Carol,* Dickens would walk the streets of London at night—ebullient, thoughtful, or rapt in a deep, inner conversation that, if you were standing nearby, you'd notice was not really that inner! If you'd like to call the angels to help with creative ideas—whether you're out walking or not—you can call Uriel, whose name means Fire of God. If you're seeking creativity for writing or communication projects, you can invoke Gabriel, as well. Here's a quick invocation to Uriel.

Invoking Creative Forces

*Angel of light, Fire of God,
Light the spark of creativity within me.
Help me discover ideas that shine
And I will do my part.*

The angels are all around us, always willing to help. Here's a very old invocation to your guardian angel, but if you'd like, you can replace the words *Angel of God* with the name of any particular angel you wish—for instance, Michael, Gabriel, Raphael, and so on.

Invoking Your Guardian Angel

*Angel of God, my guardian dear,
To whom God's love commits me here,
Ever this day be at my side,
To light, to guard, to rule, and guide.*

Lost and Found

The next invocation is something my sister and I believe to be quite magical. It's a call for help in finding lost objects, and although it's Catholic in origin, people of all faiths have always told us how successful it's been for them. The invocation is to Anthony of Padua, the patron Saint of lost objects.

There is a little story that illustrates just how powerful words can be—words that have been given even greater power by their long-term, collective use by people all over the world. I once had a phone appointment with a client named Katherine in New York City who had lost a very valuable and quite sizeable diamond ring. When we first started our session, she shared her concern about the ring, and I asked if she knew about the invocation to St. Anthony. She told me she was Catholic and, although she had never heard of this particular prayer, she had already done four Novenas, totaling 36 days of prayer to St. Anthony in order to find the ring. In spite of that, I encouraged her to recite the invocation below, telling her that I always find whatever I'm looking for when I say this very magical prayer—which is true!

Invocation to Find Lost Objects

Dear St. Anthony, come around,
Something's lost and can't be found.

I said this once to her and had her repeat it with me. After she did, she said, "Wait a minute. I want to get a pen and write this down."

She pulled open the pencil drawer of the desk where she sat, and there was her diamond ring! She had looked to no avail in that drawer *many* times over during her search, but there it was now. Katherine was ecstatic. After her squeals of delight subsided, she asked why her prayers to Anthony hadn't worked. I told her they had worked! They helped her find me, which helped her find the invocation.

I'm convinced that good old Tony—as those of us who speak to him often call him—will not only help you find your stuff, but will also move it for you if necessary! The key lies in the enormous power these words have carried for generations.

Some people who may be concerned with the word *can't,* change it to *must.* I have found, after a lifetime of using the original *can't,* that it works just fine, but use whichever word feels right for you.

Don't dismiss this. When something goes missing, give this quick, little invocation a try. Simply keep repeating it—out loud or to yourself—as you're looking for anything lost or misplaced. You may find yourself suddenly thinking about a certain room or area. When you do, go and look there. You'll be amazed by how it works!

Who Ya Gonna Call?

As you can see, there are lots of energies, qualities, histories, natural forces, and individuals that you can invoke for myriad reasons. But of all those you call, don't forget to call yourself—your higher mind, your inner will, your own eternal being. When you call yourself, you can find your joy, you can tap your power, and you can link yourself to God.

Actually, you've already been invoking yourself and your own energy through most of the Trigger Words we've used in this book. From shifting your posture, to engaging more deeply with loved ones, to sleeping better, to accessing your power, all Trigger Words are invocations. They call to action, to your purpose, to your energies, to you! Here's an invocation that combines with a declaration to lift you to the heights of happiness.

Invocation to Joy

I call to my blissful spirit, the happy heart inside me.
I abandon darkness and pain, and I rise up on the wings of joy.

You can say this invocation any time, but alternative Trigger Words may be easier to use on the quick. Some of the triggers you can use are *blissful spirit, happy heart, joyful self,* or any similar phrase that sparks happiness for you. If you'd like, you can call to your *jeu d'esprit,* (pronounced "JUH des-SPREE"). It's French for a playful, joyful, or happy spirit. As you do with any Trigger Word, hold the energy and meaning deeply in your heart and mind as you say them.

Invoking the Good, Invoking God

> *"Every day I pray. I yield myself to God, tensions and anxieties go out of me, and peace and power come in."*
>
> — DALE CARNEGIE

Many of the prayers in the previous chapters invoke God—and not surprisingly so. Here is one attributed to Kahlil Gibran that can help you remember that ever-present source.

Never Alone

Each day and night I feel Your presence.
You may not be near to touch,
But You are in my mind and heart.
You meet my needs so silently,
I am never alone because of You.

As a trigger to remember this energy quickly, you can use *God within, never alone, divinity here, divine heart,* or just one of the lines from this poem. With this, and with any process, prayer, or invocation, you can make your own Trigger Word. The easier it is to insert throughout your day, the more of that energy will permeate your life. And what a life it could be when filled with Divine presence, power, and happiness!

Chapter 14

HEALING PRAYERS

"O Lord my God, I cried to you and you have healed me."

— PSALMS 30:3

There have been so many studies illustrating the positive impact that prayer has in healing that it is a wonder why prayer isn't prescribed as an ancillary treatment for almost every condition! A double-blind study done by Randolph Byrd at San Francisco General Hospital tested various outcomes of coronary-care patients. It showed that those who received prayer did significantly better than the control group receiving the same fine medical treatment without prayer.

In another study at Duke University, Dr. Mitch Krucoff compared five groups of coronary patients, all of whom received the same medical treatment. Other than the control group, all of the other groups received other therapies. Two received relaxation training and imagery training, respectively. One group was given therapeutic touch, and the last group was prayed for by others. The groups who received the other three modalities saw a 20 to 30 percent reduction in complications over the control group. The group who was prayed for had a reduction of 50 percent in heartbeat abnormalities and a whopping 100 percent reduction in heart failure and heart attacks!

Healings We Can See but Can't Understand

If you'd like to get an actual picture of what healing prayer can do, go back to Emoto's book *The Hidden Messages in Water.* There you'll find pictures of lake water crystals taken before and after a healing prayer had been said by a Buddhist priest. The difference is astonishing.

Why do prayers work in healing? The answer to that is unknown. Is it because prayers are sent to a higher being who intervenes? Perhaps. Or maybe healing prayers spoken on behalf of an individual simply end up sending good, life affirming energy to that person. It's easy to speculate about many possible reasons why prayer might assist in healing, but it would only be speculation. The precise answer to why healing prayers work is unknown and unknowable. Sadly, in this modern age of science, reason, and immediate access to worldwide information, too many people are unwilling to consider the uncertain and the unknowable as even possible.

> *"Penetrating so many secrets,*
> *we cease to believe in the unknowable.*
> *But there it sits, nevertheless, calmly licking its chops."*
>
> — H. L. MENCKEN

H. L. Mencken may be implying that if you actively avoid the unknowable or uncertain, it could just end up biting you in the butt. To avoid it in the case of healing prayer, you might be dismissing a great opportunity to support you in your wellness.

The Prayers of Others

All of the studies already mentioned have been about the effects of remote prayer, where those needing healing were prayed for by others. It's important to note that those praying for the healing of others were not told what or how to pray. The type of prayers ran the gamut from Christian to Buddhist and everything in between.

If you'd like to receive a healing through prayer, there are hundreds, and perhaps thousands, of healing prayer groups of different religions around the world. And since the type of prayer or religion doesn't matter, you can avail yourself of all the prayer groups you'd like.

Of course, if you're going to be prayed for, you can reciprocate by praying for all those who are on their prayer lists as well. If you do, you'll be sending healing to them and to you. Research at the University of Michigan by Neal Krause showed that those who prayed for others experienced a reduction in stress and an improvement in health and well-being themselves. What better proof is there that good energy expands everywhere?!

Praying for Yourself

Just like Power Words, prayers are more effective the more strongly you believe in them—and in you. Some studies show that many people believe their own prayers would be less effective in their healing than prayers by others. So, when you pray for yourself, believe in yourself and in your prayers.

The next important component in healing prayer—as in working with Power Words—is how much you emotionally link to the words you say. Medical researcher Herbert Benson of Harvard University studied the effects of prayer and meditation on a number of very divergent groups of people, including Catholics, Protestants, and Jews. Some used single words (such as words that mean "one" or "peace") and some used prayerful phrases, such as the first line of a favorite psalm, prayer, or biblical passage. All of the various forms were successful in bringing healthy changes to the body, as long as they were continued. Those that used more emotionally engaging prayers found it easier to commit to a long-term program, and therefore had more continued success.

Striking a Perfect Balance

> *"All the art of living lies in a fine mingling*
> *of letting go and holding on."*
>
> — HAVELOCK ELLIS

Two different studies (Yujiro Ikemi with the Kyusher University School of Medicine in Japan and Spindrift, Inc., in Salem, Oregon) indicate that an important factor in healing and in healing prayer is that of surrender. Non-directed prayer occurs when one lets go and asks only for the highest and best—or, indeed, to allow and support the will of God. Even without focus on a specific outcome, great benefit can occur. It's important to note, however, that other studies on directed prayer in which very specific outcomes were visualized (Dr. G. Richard Smith at the University of Arkansas and Dr. Howard Hall of Pennsylvania State University) also showed significant success.

The findings on non-directed and directed approaches are another indication of how effective many diverse types of prayer can be. Striking a balance between letting go and taking action in life can also help in your healing. Here are some other factors that some studies found helpful in healing. They're also very helpful in a life of mental, emotional, and physical wellness.

A Self-Empowered Life for Wellness

1. Maintain a spiritual perspective that broadens your reality beyond the physical and personal world.

2. Hold a sense of purpose that resonates to your spiritual will. Pursue activities that contribute to others and that promote your happiness and spiritual growth.

3. Develop the ability to relax, release stress, focus, and visualize—in other words, *meditate.* Of course,

relaxation will require some sense of surrender, while focusing and visualizing will promote the specific outcome you seek. It's a great way to bring together the non-directed and directed approaches.

4. Hold a positive outlook and an attitude of inner love and power, both of which can be supported by your prayers, Trigger Words, and Lifting Words.

5. Keep learning. Discover new ideas about every part of your life and your world. You are the most important job you'll ever have.

If you can bring all of these forces together while living a prayerful life, you will be well on your way to joyful health. If you'd like to find out more about the many studies on prayer, take a look at the books *Healing Words* and *Prayer Is Good Medicine,* both by Larry Dossey, M.D.; *Love & Survival* by Dean Ornish, M.D.; and Dr. Bernie Siegel's book *Love, Medicine & Miracles.* Of course, Louise Hay's *You Can Heal Your Life* can also give you great insight into the mind-body connection in healing. There are also many prayer books, websites, and newsletters that can provide you with prayers to help you with every aspect of your life—from healing to selling your home. You can discover some prayers for yourself—and even write some of your own. Here are some of my favorites to help get you started.

Spiritualist Healing Prayer

Spiritualism is one of the few religions in the world where healing is a part of their regular church service. Any member of the congregation can choose to receive a healing each and every week. If you ever find yourself in Lily Dale, New York, the world's largest and oldest Spiritualist community, don't miss the service at the Healing Temple there. It's a profound experience.

The following is a healing prayer used in Spiritualist churches around the world. I really like this prayer.

Spiritualist Prayer for Healing

I ask the Great Unseen Healing Force
to remove all obstructions from my mind and body
and to restore me to perfect health.

I ask this in all sincerity and honesty
and I will do my part.

I ask this Great Unseen Healing Force
to help both present and absent ones
who are in need of help
and to restore them to perfect health.

I put my trust in the love and power of God.

I know a woman, Amy, who had been diagnosed with breast cancer. She was due to have surgery on a Wednesday, and she decided to spend the weekend before that going to the Spiritualist services and to the Healing Temple at Lily Dale. The above prayer was used at the services and given to her at the Healing Temple, where she received healing and meditated twice a day. When Amy went to the hospital the following Tuesday for her pre-op tests and scans, all of the cancer was gone, and the surgery was cancelled.

Now I don't believe that only one factor created Amy's spontaneous remission. There were many factors that came together for Amy that weekend. This prayer was one of them—though I'm sure the extraordinary energies at the Healing Temple did their part, too! (For more information about Lily Dale, go to www .lilydaleassembly.com.)

Hebrew Healing Prayers

Here are a few prayers, including one from the Old Testament that harkens back to ancient times. Happily you can use modern times to find similar prayers by going to www.jewishealing.com and many other websites.

Old Testament Healing Prayer

Heal me, O Lord, and I shall be healed;
save me, and I shall be saved,
for you are my praise.

— JEREMIAH **17:14**

With the following prayer you can invoke healing for yourself or for others. Of course, you can do that with most of these prayers and invocations by simply naming and holding a loving focus on that person, family, or group of your choice.

Mi Sheberach

May the One who blessed our ancestors, Sarah and Abraham,
bless [insert name here] along with all of the ill among us.
God, let your spirit rest upon all who are ill and comfort them.
May they and we soon know a time of complete healing,
and let us say, Amen.

The next is a brief Jewish prayer shown in two languages. This is an excellent little invocation that can be said any time throughout your day in those moments when the longer prayers, or the time to say them, may not be available to you.

Healing Invocation

El na refa na lah.
Please God, bring healing.

I have a friend named Isaac, who has long suffered from a depleted immune system. He was prone to infections and seemed to be constantly on antibiotics, which made him very tired. He began to say the previous prayer frequently, but without urgency, as he went through his day. He also began to meditate daily. Over time his infections began to diminish, and his energy returned. He still gets a sinus or ear infection once in a while, but most of his days are now lived in happy—and energetic—health!

Healing Specific Conditions

Here are a few prayers that allow you to focus on particular conditions.

> *O Lord, may your hand be upon me and heal me of*
> *[insert name of condition here].*
> *Also, please bring healing to all who suffer from this condition.*
> *May peace and wellness thrive within me, through your glory. Amen.*

Prayer for Mental and Emotional Health

> *Dear God, when I am troubled, help me to know only compassion and love.*
> *Grant for me tranquility of body, mind, and heart,*
> *and I will seek serenity and peace in every feeling and thought. Amen.*

Calling the Angel of Healing

Raphael is an angel of a great many gifts. He is the patron of love (as seen in the last chapter), marriage, travel, and most of all healing. Here is a prayer that can help you invoke this wonderful archangel's powers.

Invocation to Archangel Raphael for Healing

> *Archangel Raphael, send*
> *your healing to _____*
> *and bring a full recovery to him/her.*
> *Angel of Health, we trust in you and rest*
> *in the confidence of your aid. Amen.*

Healing Forces Abound

We have seen the Spiritualist prayer that invokes the Great Unseen Healing Force as well as Navaho and Apache invocations to the universal forces of life. Nature is constantly trying to bring balance to itself, and that balancing tendency is natural in your body as well. Here's an invocation to those balancing forces that abound within and around you.

Invoking Natural Healing Energies

May the forces of healing
and balance in nature
come to me,
bringing balance and harmony
through every system
and cell within me. I balance my mind,
body, and spirit in harmony.
And I live in joyful health.

Trusting in Hopeful Expectation

Whatever prayer you wish to utilize is up to you. All you have to do is believe in yourself, believe in prayer and invocation, and live with purpose and trust.

Pray for yourself, pray for others, and ask others to pray for you. Let go of urgency, and remember, trust in the healing power of your prayers. Some studies show that there was greater healing when doctors shared hopeful expectations with their patients. Let yourself live in the hopeful expectation that your prayers shall help to bring you only wellness, grace, and good in body, mind, and heart. Know it and expect it to be so.

*"There is no medicine like hope, no incentive so great,
and no tonic so powerful as expectation of something tomorrow."*

— ORISON S. MARDEN

Words of Wellness

Of course, if you want good health, it's imperative that your life be filled with good words. Living in toxicity won't ever support a life of wellness.

I had a friend, Todd, a wonderful and gentle man, whose wife spent most of her waking life in bitter complaint—talking incessantly about what's wrong with the neighbors, friends, roads, work, government, church, waitress, postman, everything. People who knew her would take extreme measures to avoid running into her when they were out. But poor Todd, who didn't like confrontation, suffered in all-too-tolerant silence. Ultimately, her negative words weren't the only things that affronted Todd's ears. In one ear he also developed cancer. His wife's words had become physically toxic to him. Luckily, the cancer was surgically removed, and Todd lived many more years, passing much later in old age. Perhaps he listens to angelic voices now.

I don't know if there could be a more literal example of the harmful effects of negative words. In Part IV we'll take a deeper look at limiting language and how to lift it to create a higher reality. But where your health is concerned, there is one guiding principle: *Being well is born from well-being.*

So, fill yourself with a sense of well-being. Speak well of yourself and others. And require those around you to do so as well. Be sure to treat yourself well, too. Sanctify your life with prayers and with powerful words. When you do, your experience won't just be holy, but will also be wholly well.

Part IV

LIFTING WORDS FOR AN ELEVATED LIFE

"Lord, we know what we are,
but know not what we may be."

— WILLIAM SHAKESPEARE

Chapter 15

Looking at Limiting Language

"The only devils in the world are those running in our own hearts.
That is where the battle should be fought."

— Mahatma Gandhi

The story of your life is written in all of the words you use—not only the words you say, but also the words you think. Words carry energy, and words cause results. In daily life many people don't really think much about what they say, but they should. Empowering thoughts and words create a powerful life, and damaging thoughts and words will damage your life.

Seeds of Pain

Most people think that painful feelings are caused only by negative people or events. But these are only the beginning seeds of pain. Once a hurtful situation occurs, many people continue to focus on their pain, causing it to grow and grow. During difficult and hurtful times, painful feelings are valid; so is using the correct words to describe them. The problem happens when those words take over, turning into an unending chorus of negativity and complaint.

Lily Tomlin said, "Man invented language to satisfy his deep need to complain." Though the great comic was probably joking, her jest rings true. When difficult times happen, they often take center stage. Many complain, not just to others, but to themselves, creating pervasive habits of negative words and limiting thought patterns. Even those who are positively minded do it more often than they realize.

You've probably heard and even said the sentiment, *That's too good to be true.* But how often have you heard, *That's too bad to be true?* It's almost as if we consider good things to be unbelievable, while we expect bad things to happen. In the future we should really think about the implications of a statement like *That's too good to be true.* Do we want to create the reality that good things shouldn't be expected? Of course not!

We must be more conscious and precise with all of our words if we really want to harness their power in our lives. We first need to consider the meanings of words and the images, histories, and feelings they call up. But, perhaps more important, we must also be very aware of the messages they send to the world.

Words Charged with Energy

Though all words are charged with energy, the phrase *emotionally charged words* describes those that carry an extra punch of vibration about them. Negatively charged words send a current of negative, dark energy that will charge your life with those qualities whenever you use those words. Conversely, positively charged words will give off currents of empowering energy everywhere throughout your life.

Frequently using self-actualizing affirmations will help to positively charge your life. But if you use negatively charged words about anything or anyone throughout your day, it will significantly counteract the positive effect of the affirmations. Whether you think or say negatively charged words about yourself, about another, about a specific situation, or even about the world at large, your life will be pulled down by their heavy energy. Regardless of what or whom they describe, it's your own energy that's affected most.

I have a client, Victoria, who had created a lifelong habit of seeing—and talking about—what was wrong with everything. As she started to become more aware, she determined to change the energy in her life. She began to say affirmations every morning and before bed. Yet all the rest of the day was spent in her regular negative vocabulary. Not seeing the results she wanted, she became very disappointed. It was only after she started taking the steps to make changes through all of her daily language (see Chapter 17 and 18) that she started to see a difference in her own energy and in her life. Now her thoughts, her words, and her life are all aligned to happiness, purpose, and fulfillment.

This is why the use of Power Words is so very important. The *whole* of your language informs and energizes your life—for good or bad. And in order to change a negative, defeated, deflated life, the words charged with negative, defeating, and deflating energy must be replaced by words that are positively charged. And so—with a nod to Tesla, the father of alternating current—in order to create an alternative life, you must alternate the current of your words to a positive charge.

Currents of Word Power

Close your eyes, and begin to imagine a current of negative energy flowing around you. Every time you use damaging words and focus on past difficult times, this current of negativity seems to grow. Take a moment to notice everything you feel physically and emotionally with this negative current within you.

Now take a deep breath and release all of that energy entirely. Let it all go. Begin to feel a current of positive energy move through you. With this positive force you may feel like your own energy is being lifted in some way. Any time you use an uplifting word or recall a joyful memory, this current of positive energy expands. Imagine this energizing current flowing into every part of you and your life. Notice how you feel with this positive energy moving through you.

During this process, you may have found the negative charge pulling you down emotionally, or even physically. When you switched to the positive current, you may have felt lighter, enthusiastic, or even a little excited. Just think of the wonderful energy that could flow through your life when you use words that carry a positive current. But in order to flip that switch, you first need to learn to release the old words that carry a dark and negative current through your language.

Words That Wound

There isn't anyone in the world who hasn't had the experience of being wounded by someone else's words. Some words take the wind out of your sails and deflate your enthusiasm. Some negate your value, and, consequently, your sense of well-being. And some can be so wounding they almost feel like a blow to the chest. It's so sad when people say wounding words to each other, but how much sadder is it when they say them to themselves?

The only good thing to come from negative words is that they're evidence of how very powerful words are. Some people think they use negative words because their lives are negative, but in truth, they keep their lives negative by using negative words. If words can destroy, they can also build. But you can only build a new language after you've demolished and excavated the old.

First, start to recognize the real and implied meaning in everything you say. Also, widen your scope to a larger, long-term vision of the effects of your words. If words can have an *immediate* impact, think of the enormous impact they have when you use them over and over for years and years.

> *"The longer we dwell on our misfortunes,*
> *the greater is their power to harm us."*
>
> — VOLTAIRE

I have a friend, Carolyn Sampson, who teaches that repeating old, negative patterns and beliefs is like constantly picking at an old wound. It opens it up anew every day and never lets it heal.

If your words focus only on lack and loss, you'll generate an energy that will expand lack and loss in every corner of your life. If you question your worth, you won't be valued by yourself or anyone else. Some people might justify their negativity saying, "But it's true. Nobody loves me; I screw everything up. Emptiness is my only history." Well, if those are the only words spoken or thought, it will be the only truth known—until new words are chosen. Your history is a measure of only one thing: your history. No matter what you were taught or what you've experienced, you can shift that energy. The words you choose now are the measure of the truth you want.

Revising History

Can words actually change history? Just ask teachers of the Civil War. Gettysburg was not a monument to heroism; it was a corpse-filled killing field. It was a scene of such military folly and resulting slaughter that the generals on both sides—Meade and Lee—submitted their resignations. But with Lincoln's powerful 276-word speech, that battle in American history was changed in people's minds. Forever.

> *"Lincoln's [Gettysburg] address vividly*
> *demonstrates the generative power of words:*
> *the power of words not simply to describe realty, but to create it."*
>
> — HARRY BECKWITH

The Gettysburg Address did not change the great loss suffered in that battle. It changed the perspective people had of it, and therefore their responses to it, and to the war. The events of those three days weren't changed; they were revised.

The root word for *revise* comes from the Latin *videre,* which means *to see.* Because of Lincoln's address, the Battle of Gettysburg was re-seen. You, too, can create a *re*-vision, a *re*-image, and a *re*-statement of your history—which can make significant changes that can correct and improve your life. Changing your history changes your present and your potential.

The truth is, we're always changing—sometimes in ways we can't see and sometimes in ways that really show. It reminds me of one of my favorite quotes from Lewis Carroll:

> "Who are *you*?" said the Caterpillar. . . .
> Alice replied, rather shyly, "I—I hardly know, Sir, just at present—at least I know who I *was* when I got up this morning, but I think I must have been changed several times since then."

Even those people who seem deeply entrenched in negative lifelong patterns are changing every day. They are either putting themselves deeper in the trench, or they're doing something to lift themselves out of it. The opportunity for positive change is always present—even with the most seemingly fixed histories. Unlike Alice in Wonderland, you don't have to jump down a rabbit hole or step through a looking glass to make it happen.

Consider the alcoholic who now leads a successful and sober life; or the overweight person with a lifelong eating disorder who now exercises every day and motivates others to be trim and healthy, too; or the abused wife with a long history of submission who leaves her husband and becomes strong again. All these people would still be where they started, if their history defined them.

Change Up

I have a client, Mary, who wanted to accept a job offer, but it required a great deal of public speaking, which terrified her. Fear of public speaking is the most common of all fears. Almost everybody you've seen on stage, TV, giving a lecture, or leading a group, had jittery knees, butterflies, shortness of breath, or clammy hands the first several times they stepped before a crowd. And Mary was no exception. She refused to let her fear prevent her from taking the new job. She began working with many of the Trigger Words we saw in Parts II and III to free her from her fears. She also began to visualize her successful performance and practiced speaking in front of a number of small groups. Soon, her fear no longer defined her or her limitations. Her old job and her old history gave way to a new life of possibility.

I have another client, Lynne, who was agoraphobic and was housebound for over two decades. She restructured her self-talk and with home visits by a counselor and lots of behavioral practicing sessions, she now travels the world with ease.

If one's history shouldn't define an individual, then what should? Well, it may be best to not define yourself in any way—even in terms of your potential, since your greatest, long-term potential is unknown to you. If you want to define yourself in any way, do it through that part of you that is, in a word, indefinable. It's the amorphous part of self that exists beyond form or shape or measure—that part that creates ideas, that lives in a world of possibility and power eternally. It's your spirit!

Did Mary, Lynne, and all those who have broken through their limiting histories do so by defining themselves in this "measureless" way? Yes. Well, to a certain point they did. People who succeed in moving beyond their past, do so because they first change their scope. They broaden their perspective to one of greater possibility. They turn their focus from the loss and limits of yesterday to the opportunities that come with today and tomorrow. And as they change their scope, they change their language—and their actions. This change of action is an important component. You could study many books that tell you all about your measureless power and your boundless self. And you could believe that reality at an intellectual level very strongly. But if you live in an abusive relationship, maintain an addiction, don't take actions that honor you, or allow yourself to be devalued in some way, your actions will contradict your words. And your message to the world will come through your actions.

When you change your words, your new words will help you change your actions—from those that limit, lower, and dismiss to those that lift, expand, and empower. This shifts your energy and your life. You'll find that when you combine powerful words with empowering actions, there is no potential you can't achieve.

The Powerful Potential of New Words

There are those who seek to be factual with their language. Some seek to be eloquent. Both are great causes. But if you are to bring energy, joy, and benefit to your life and to the world, your language must be more than factual or eloquent. It must empower. What would the world be—what would your life be—if all your language had a positive current and sought to enlighten, to expand, to ennoble, to lift? You can find out with just a little effort and commitment. It's as easy as discovering new Lifting Words and using them.

Seeking new words doesn't only change your vocabulary, but it also changes how you see and define yourself and your world. Awareness of your words creates awareness of yourself. You begin to assess what you're saying and determine whether or not those words lift and expand your life or pull it down and oppress it.

Every word should reflect your inestimable value, power, self-honoring, joy, and compassion. At first, those types of words might feel false to you because of old thoughts and history. But remember, your past is past. What you make present now in your language and actions will inform your future.

> *"There is no material with which human beings work,*
> *which has so much potential energy as words."*

> — ERNEST ELMO CALKINS

Potent Word Power

Take a moment to close your eyes and breathe deeply. Bring inside you the words *potent* and *potential*. Feel their energy comingle within you. Say the words again and notice that you are filled with *potent* energy—so *potent* that there is no *potential* you cannot reach.

The words *potent* and *potential* come from the same root word for *power*. Your unlimited potential lies in the power to reign in the stampeding horses of your old thoughts—and lift your language with every single word. When you master your every day language, the very fiber of your life will be changed. You'll find that your potent new Lifting Words can take you to boundless potential and success.

Chapter 16

Expletives Deleted— Moving from Swearing to Blessings

"Moods don't last. It is their chief charm."

— Oscar Wilde

Everyone invokes both good and bad energies every day. Some words are said with intention, yet some are spontaneous and unconscious. The custom of invoking negative and dark energies is practiced by a great many people. I'm not speaking about witch-craft and pentacles painted on the floor here—the dark types of invocation to which I'm referring is the all-too-common practice of swearing. Sometimes, when people are in a bad mood, they're quick to vent those feelings in a barrage of swear words. But they can help end a bad mood more quickly by changing those words to ones of a higher energy, if they think it's important enough to do so.

For most people, the act of swearing is a simple and innocu-ous opportunity to vent their anger and frustrations. But it may not be as harmless as they think. Every word that is voiced has power to it, and negative words can carry a negative force that may surprise you.

Of course, everyone has feelings, and there are many times when it's valid to feel frustrated and angry. It's also valid to express those feelings. But if your expression of those feelings is always a litany of damnation, it may be your own energy that you are damning. Such words really do carry a great deal of frustration, anger, and malevolence abroad into the world. They increase those feelings within and around you, spreading it to the events and people in your life.

The word *damn* means *to condemn, to curse,* and even *to cause the ruin of.* If you say, "Damn it," when you get frustrated with a difficult situation, then you're actually voicing a desired intention to condemn that situation. Your energy will be *filled* with the agitated color of red, which is the natural color both of the word *damn* and of the anger you're feeling. This red will increase the agitation in and around you, bringing your voiced condemnation back on yourself. Certainly, that is something you don't want to do.

There are many "venting" words that carry darkness, agitation, and difficult energy. Would you really want to surround yourself, your work, or your home with the energy or color of fecal matter? Well, you do when you use the words *shit* or *crap.*

Crappy Word Power

Take a moment now to close your eyes and think of the word *shit* or *crap.* Choose one, and hold it in your mind and energy. Really fill your whole being with *shit* or *crap.* Notice how you feel. Notice that your energy feels heavy, sludgy, and—well—*crappy.*

Now see if you can go a step further and imagine putting the word *shit* in your mouth. Really take a moment to imagine it. How appalling! Consider the effects of spreading such intentions and energy all over the issues and people in your life—not very tasteful for anyone!

Now let all of that go. Send that word and that energy completely away with your next exhalation. Bring the word *sunlight* inside you just to clear and lift your energy. Feel yourself filled with bright, golden warmth and light. Every dark and muddy corner has been lit by the light of the sun. Notice how much better you feel being alight and happy instead of *crappy.* Make a commitment to release "crappy" words from your vocabulary.

What a difference between *shit* and *sunlight!* I'm not recommending that you use *sunlight* as a replacement for swearing. But you could certainly use it any time you want to clear out crappy feelings and let in the light!

In another example, consider the habit many people have of referring to things—or even other people—as a "pain in the neck." This projects an *actual* expectation of pain. And you certainly don't want to voice the intention of creating pain—in the neck or butt or anywhere else. I once had a client whose father was often angry and always expressed his frustration by saying, "What a pain in the ass!" It was his lifelong mantra—until he died of colon cancer.

Of course, it's important to give yourself permission for your own self-expression. You can't live your life as a word-Nazi, fearing or condemning yourself for voicing every negative word. That would only add guilt and judgment to the energy already there. But you *can* bring a higher consciousness and loving intention to your choice of words.

For instance, though *darn* is merely a euphemism for *damn,* it also means *to mend* or *repair.* By making the change from damn to *darn,* you're actually voicing the intention to repair the frustrating element rather than condemn it. This change may seem like a weak substitute, but actually it's far more powerful in the results it will produce—especially if you use it as a Trigger Word to immediately put your focus on fixing the situation. From now on try to make the switch in your words from damn to *darn,* and you'll trigger the actions you need to take to the fix the problem. In this way more "damnable" situations can be repaired than you might think.

Switching a swearing habit when difficulty strikes is a change worth making. It's my belief in the profound power of words—not in some severe moral code—that causes me to replace swear words with new words. For example, sometimes I try to replace *Oh my*

God! With *Oh my goodness!* This, then, reminds me to find the goodness in that moment, and it changes my mood and my focus immediately. It really is possible to find goodness if you look for it!

I also like to turn the "f" word into *flip.* Like *darn,* the word *flip* carries the positive connotation of flipping the situation around. When I say *flip,* it reminds me to see the situation in a better light and with new results. You can say both *darn* and *flip* with as much force as you might have said the originals; only this time you will be placing constructive—not destructive—energy around you, and around the experience itself. Let's take a moment to give it a try.

Flipping Word Power

Close your eyes and think of an event that might trigger the word f--k in your mind or speech. Maybe your car won't start, or your computer breaks, or you're stuck in traffic and missing an important meeting, or something even more problematic.

In your imagination, put yourself in the scene. Let yourself really feel the frustration and the urge to say f--k. Imagine yourself beginning to say it. Then replace that word with the word *flip.* Strongly repeat *flip* several times in a row so that you can infuse that word with energy. Begin to see that situation immediately flipping around to a better conclusion. Truly see the situation flip in every way. Notice how much better you feel—more focused, more positive, more assured of your ability to correct the situation. There is benefit to come, and you feel really optimistic about it.

With this process you can see how you can change your focus from what went wrong to what good you can do. Every time you change a swear word to a word of benefit, you change the energy around the situation.

I had a friend, Melinda, who told me that she loved saying the word *f--k*. She said it was the best way to vent any extreme feelings she had—from frustration to anger. She was sure that anything that allowed you to vent in that way had to be a good thing.

I wanted to give her a firsthand experience of the real energy of that word, so I showed her how to muscle test it. I asked her to raise one of her arms and hold it out straight and stiff, resisting me as I pushed down on it. She was actually very strong and resisted the pressure well.

Then I told her to do the same thing again, only this time to say the word *f--k* first. When I put even the slightest pressure on her stiff, outstretched arm, it easily fell back to her side. Her jaw dropped with surprise. She had the evidence she needed to see how weak that word made her. And if saying it only once zapped her strength so much, what was happening to her physical stamina when she used it dozens of times a day? (You and a friend can use this muscle-testing process to discover what this word or any word does to your energy.)

Melinda started to curtail her use of *f--k* in her daily life, replacing it with *flip* and other options. She didn't want to have a weakened system at any level. That word was significantly entrenched in her daily vocabulary, so breaking the habit took her a long time. But she told me that the less she used that word—and some of the other negative words she used to say—the more energy she had. She didn't have to sleep as much, and she had lots more vitality!

So don't dismiss these changes as simplistic or unrealistic. There's an undercurrent of redirection that comes with your choice. Goodness brings the energy of love and peace. And even more important, the words *darn* and *flip* will voice your intention—and put your attention into mending and switching the situation at hand. Instead of losing energy with swearing, these new words of power bring more power and more options to you. And if you can use new words for swearing, you can find new words for everything!

Swear to God!

There are so many different variations of so many different swear words, they could fill a book of their own. What's important is for you to stay fully aware of the energy of all words before you use them. Swear words—like every other word—not only express energy, but they also invoke more of that kind of energy to come back to you. All words communicate *and* invite. What a strange double message we send during those times when we use spiritual words to swear, like *Holy shit* or *God damn*.

There are times you might want to use the word *holy.* I personally think *Holy Cow* makes a great blessing at meals. It recognizes the grace of your food and invites a great steak to come your way! But regardless of all the *Holy Cows* and *Holy Toledos,* using the word *God* requires deliberation.

We've already seen the greater meaning of damn and how it carries the energy of condemnation to those who use it. Consider the implications when you say, "God damn it," or "God damn you." Invoking a divine energy to bring condemnation and ruin to a situation or person can be an extreme misuse of energy. Take a moment to sit with those statements and feel their energy. There really is a sense of wrongness about them.

So let yourself release the habit of using the word God when you're angry. Anger and the other lower emotions of the ego are contrary to your spirit, which is where your divinity lies. If you want to invoke God's energy while you're angry or upset, let it be a call for peace and understanding. Those qualities will serve you much better at such times.

Some people use the word God during times of surprise: *Good God* or *Good Lord.* Some also say *good gracious* or *my heavens.* I think these may be good choices at times, because they affirm goodness.

Regardless of how you would use the word *God,* be sure to treat it as you would all of the empowering words you choose. Feel its energy in your heart and know the forces you are bringing to yourself and to your world. When you lovingly hold *God* inside you, how can you go wrong?

Blessing Difficult Times

In Chapter 13 we talked about bringing *blessings* to yourself and others. But there are other opportunities to say "God bless you," when pleasant thoughts are more distant than turbulent ones. When situations disappoint you or difficult people darken your day, *bless you* may not be the first thing on your lips. But it might be one of the best triggers of all.

> *"And blessings on the falling out*
> *That all the more endears,*
> *When we fall out with those we love*
> *and kiss again with tears."*

> — ALFRED, LORD TENNYSON

Often, when thoughts of someone who has hurt or judged you come to mind, the first response is anger, defensiveness, or judgments of your own. In previous chapters we've looked into a number of Trigger Words that help override such patterns and free you from such thoughts. Wishing *blessings* upon those who may have judged you or hurt you can be as big a blessing to you as to them. It not only helps you to break your train of negative thought, but it also helps you invoke a higher experience of peace to all involved, giving you a new perspective and a greater ease in letting go.

Looking for the Silver Lining

> *"Ye fearful saints fresh courage take,*
> *The clouds ye so much dread*
> *Are big with mercy, and shall break*
> *In blessings on your head."*

> — WILLIAM COWPER

Another opportunity to use the word *blessings* comes during those times when disappointments seem to darken the horizon. It can turn any obstacle into the promise of an opportunity.

Blessing Word Power Here

Close your eyes and imagine yourself at a point where a hindrance seems to cloud your path, or another person has hurt you. At first you may feel sad, disappointed, or confused, but you take a deep breath and declare to yourself, *There is a blessing here.* And even if you can't find it immediately, you declare, *I will find the blessings here.* And you will seek them out. Put yourself at the ready to see and embrace the shower of *blessings* coming your way. They may be disguised in an unfortunate event, but they *are* there. And you can find them when you simply declare, *I find a blessing here.*

You can stop eruptions of negativity by changing swear words to Power Words with new perspectives. Change your swearing to blessings and lift the energy for all concerned. Say, "God bless you," and invite Divine comforts to another. Or simply say, "Bless you," to invoke the qualities of grace, good fortune, and happiness to that person. When you use these phrases to heal an angry moment or relationship, the resulting energy is laced with high intention and brings goodwill to yourself and to the world.

Chapter 17

DECONSTRUCTING
THE OLD LANGUAGE

*"The person who moves a mountain begins
by carrying away small stones."*

— CHINESE PROVERB

In one sense, it may seem easy to change negative energy words to positive ones—it just requires making a choice. But for most people, it can actually be pretty difficult because they are so deeply entrenched in the habit of their old language. Changing a word habit that permeates your life might feel like moving a mountain, but you can do it by taking small steps—just like carrying one small stone away at a time.

There are a few steps necessary in reshaping an old habit—and an old language into a new one. Your commitment and a strong intention to make your life better are the tools in taking these steps.

Steps to Leave the Old Language Behind

1. Create an awakened consciousness.
2. Link your intention and will to your words.
3. Change your words immediately.
4. Keep deleting and repeating!

These steps are the building blocks of change for every part of your life. With your words you will change thoughts, emotions, and even behaviors. Each of these steps is an important part of manifesting successful results. Let's take a look.

1. Create an Awakened Conscious

Begin by bringing a new consciousness to the patterns in your words. Whether in your mundane moments or your deepest inner reflections, your words and thoughts can often be habitual. And when life happens at such accelerated speeds, most people tend to just rush through the day on automatic pilot with their words and thoughts on automatic pilot, too.

> *"One must certainly be careful how the word is spoken because when it is spoken, it creates an awesome power. We speak, and the words are life, they are material and substantive."*
>
> — MOLEFI KETE ASANTE

Words often run through life in rivers of undirected thought. You can only begin to switch the currents in your speech and thoughts by taking time throughout your day to notice the words you use in different situations. These moments of observation will shine a light on the habits you want to change and on the intentions you are making known to the world.

If you build a habit of consciousness, you will not only identify old negative words, but you can also explore—in that moment—the actual energy of those words. When you speak or think a word, feel the energy of the word as you've been doing throughout the book. Look for the underlying meaning; feel the energy it expresses; and realize the statement it makes to yourself and to the world. Determine if each word truly expresses your highest intention and will.

2. Link Your Intention and Will to Your Words

Your words are a statement of your intention, even when you don't *consciously intend* them to be so. And if that's the case, you have to be aware of what intention you're voicing to the world. Your body, your friends, your energy, and the whole world all believe every word you think and say. Most important, *you* believe every word you think and say.

There are some difficult times when we use some pretty dark words about ourselves and our lives. Some of the worst words we say about ourselves occur when we're feeling victimized. Perhaps someone has intentionally or unintentionally injured or neglected us. Or perhaps we've come upon financial difficulties or career disappointments. During such times, we use lots of different negative words. But no matter which words we use, the undercurrent those words carry is: *Poor me.* This kind of victim mentality is still present in our words even though most of us never actually use the words *poor me.* Any reference to how much we've been wounded; how hard we have it; how easily others succeed; how much we need; how little we have; how lonely we are; or any other sentiment of that ilk can all be distilled into two words: *Poor me.*

Realize that all the "poor me" types of words that you say to yourself or others are not just descriptions; they're proclamations of what you believe to be true. But do you want such desperation to be true? Your words must reflect your real intention. And little changes can make a big difference. A statement like "I don't have a good job or a happy relationship" could accurately end with the words *poor me.* But statements like, "I'm finding a good job and attracting a great relationship," could end with *powerful me.* If words are binding contracts to your truth, which of those contracts would you like to sign? If you wouldn't sign your name to it, don't speak it or think it. Act as if your words were truly a binding contract to your will—because, indeed, they are.

Writing a Contract in Word Power

Close your eyes, and recall a time when things weren't going well and you were feeling sorry for yourself. Think of the negative words you'd use. Now think the words, *Poor Me*. Even if that's not the precise diminishing or lowering phrase you would use when feeling put upon, it is the conclusion of those victimized words. Say *Poor Me* to yourself again. Now imagine those words written on a contract. It is a contract that binds you both to that state of being and to the actions that support it. Know that whenever you say any words of victimization and dismissiveness, they bind you to a contract of *Poor Me* over and over.

Imagine seeing your *Poor Me* contract before you. Do you want to sign it, or would you like to change the words first? Now change the words on your contract to *Powerful Me*. It's a contract you'd be happy to sign! Imagine yourself doing so. Make a commitment to use these words—or other positive, potent words like *Confident Me, Joyful Me, Strong Me*—often, especially during low points. It will reverse your perspective and give you a new contract that will happily renew itself every time you speak of yourself with power.

This little process may seem like a simple vignette that illustrates how powerful your words are, but it's so much more than that. There's a binding causality from the words you use to the feelings, behaviors, and actions that follow. Continued patterns of any type of words will promote their continued consequences— whether good or bad. *Since your words are contracts that bind; don't make a pledge to pain. Instead, bind yourself in a contract to joy.*

I have a client named Ralph who had a very difficult time breaking his negative word habit. I gave him the assignment of writing a contract—only a few sentences—binding himself to living in the energy of each and every negative word. I told him to do this for a week. He said that the first few days he wrote a lot of contracts with horrible energy.

It reminded him of the time as a teenager his dad made him smoke a whole pack of cigarettes to get him to quit. It worked. And so did those negative word *contracts*. He got so sick of all the negative energy he was binding to his life, he started trading the bad words for the good. He loved making contracts with good words. He started to make a simple contract with a different uplifting, empowering word every morning. He used that word as a focus for his day, and his whole life changed. People noticed the difference in his energy, and so did a certain co-worker named Linda, who is now his fiancée!

The impact of the contract between your words and your will is significant. So try making word contracts yourself. You won't just believe your words; you'll determine your actions—or lack of action—by them. Become fully aware that your words express your will. And make another contract with yourself—one that states the next time you use words that don't meet your highest intention, you'll immediately change them.

3. Change Your Words Immediately

*"To change one's life: Start immediately.
Do it flamboyantly. No exceptions."*

— WILLIAM JAMES

Of course, it's not possible to change a deeply indoctrinated pattern of negative thinking simply by saying, "I'm not going to think that anymore." Your mind just seems to have a mind of its own, driven by the force of history and habit. Sometimes thoughts are like stampeding horses, running off at the slightest provocation.

If a word, phrase, or idea is something you've used for years, it will continue to jump back into your mind, unbidden. When that happens, change it. All negative words need to be changed at the time that you use them—or as soon after as possible. Unfortunately, it may take time to realize that you had used an old negative word. But no matter how long it takes for you to catch the slip, it's imperative that you change the word as soon as you become aware of it—even if it's hours later. The more you practice replacing an old unwanted word with a new, well-intentioned one, the more you'll close the gap in time, and eventually your new, optimistic response will become your spontaneous reaction. Like a computer, your most often used words will be the first on the menu.

4. Keep Deleting and Repeating!

In many ways the mind actually does work very much like a computer. *Garbage in, garbage out* easily describes the condition of letting old words define you—the very condition we're trying to correct. When changing an old, limiting language to words that lift your life, the first mental button you'll have to push is *Delete.*

If you were working in a word document on your computer, you'd have to delete an incorrect word or phrase before typing a new one. You can do the same thing when changing words in your mind. If you actively say the word *delete,* you'll be affirming the intention to no longer use that word—erasing it, as it were, from the page. You can choose to say *delete* aloud, but saying it to yourself works just as well.

I've been making this an active part of retraining my brain. Whether it's with words of anger, self-doubt, swearing, or words of any other diminutive or dark energy, I always try to remember to command, *Delete, Delete, Delete.* Then I replace the deleted word or phrase with a beneficial one. For instance, sometimes if I misplace my keys, I may find myself exclaiming, "I keep losing stuff!" But this isn't an intention I want to support. So, now, if that statement ever comes to mind, I immediately say, *Delete, Delete, Delete.* And then I proclaim, *I find everything with ease.* This step of replacing the negative word or phrase with a positive one is key. The only way to end an old habit of words is to replace them with new ones. And those new words need to be repeated and repeated.

Repetition of the new words invokes more of the energy that you want to make true. Time and time again, it makes those words become your reality—even if at first you don't believe they are so. Keeping a journal helps you to recognize your patterns and options. It may be one of the most significant tools in your self-discovery, and it's a crucial component in changing old words to new.

Go with Me

There is a phrase in Latin, *vade mecum* (in English pronounced "VAH-deh MAY-kuum"), which literally means *go with me*. It refers to a little book or other tool that is carried for frequent reference or use. It can be an expense receipt book a laptop, or—best yet—a journal to help you lift your language.

To use journaling most effectively in word change, it would be best to carry a small, pocket-sized notebook with you throughout the day. You can also use your iPad or smartphone. When you find yourself thinking or saying a negative, sabotaging word or phrase, take a moment to put it in your *go with me*. Then write down any positive options that you can use to replace it. Do this whenever you realize you've used a defeating word, even if that realization is several minutes or hours later. Sometimes you may find yourself repeating the same old word and thought patterns for several minutes or hours, or if it's a long-held pattern, it may crop up for weeks or months! No matter how long it takes or how much repetition you find, keep writing the old words down along with their replacements. This will cement your action for change as you delete and repeat using your journal.

Of course, there are going to be times when you can't do this exercise, such as during a meeting, driving a car, or being otherwise occupied. Even if you can't do the writing, at least make the effort to change the words mentally. Later, when you get the chance, be sure to follow up with the writing exercise. It might seem that all of this effort may be a little too much work. But it's not something you need to do forever; it's just until you have started to build the new pattern.

Remember, the effort you make—or don't make—speaks volumes to yourself and to the world. You don't want to give yourself and the world the message that you're not worth the time and effort to make a great life. That's what happens when you don't take time or make an effort for yourself. When you do take action on your own behalf, you send the message that you *are* worth the time and effort. Then you'll attract the people who will make an effort for you.

Even if you start slowly with this, be persistent. If you change a negative pattern to a positive one a few times one day, then more times the next day, and even more times the next, you'll be well on your way to a successful and permanent lift in your energy and in your life. Like a stone mason building a new house where an old one once stood, you'll deconstruct the old language and prepare yourself to build a new powerful foundation in your words and your life.

Well-Lighted Words

Your words are so much more than just fleeting expressions of your thoughts in any given moment. They're invocations—calls for action to a waiting world. Like ringing a bell, your words simultaneously announce who you are while calling people and situations to you.

Your most often repeated words and themes will fill your energy, and that energy will act like a neon sign to the world. If you frequently speak and think words of joy, you will glow with the light of the sun, inviting warm, joyful, and well-lit people and situations. But, as we've seen, if your words are dark, they will only draw more darkness to you.

There are a number of Power Words and declarations that can help you bring light when things get dark. I really like the biblical quote from Genesis, "Let there be light." I use it as a command when I want to create a new and brighter perspective. Here's how you can, too. (And if you ever need an alternate, you can use the Latin, *fiat lux*, pronounced "FEE-aht LUX.")

Well-Lit Word Power

Close your eyes and bring to mind a situation that has darkened your emotional experience in some way. Large or small—whatever the situation is—begin to recall it and the people involved. Now remember some of the words that you may have used: *mad, hard, angry, hurt, worried,* or any other word that comes to mind. Hold this word and notice the darkening you feel in your emotions and the lowering of your energy.

Take a deep breath, and let that go. Now say the command, *Let there be light!* Immediately imagine this situation being flooded with light. See light go into every corner. This radiance also triggers an influx of lightened feelings and words—*joy, forgiveness, warm, excited.* You feel light fill your heart, your experience, and your energy. Say *Let there be Light!—fiat lux*—to yourself again. As soon as you do, there is light everywhere—inside and out! This command brings a new perspective and a happy release of any darkening in mind or heart. Whenever you command, *Let there be light,* there will be light in every part of your life!

Chapter 18

Lifting Words
for a Language
and Life of Bliss

"The power of words is woven so tightly into our daily lives that we hardly ever take time to marvel at it."

— HOWARD RHEINGOLD

How much more careful would you be if you could see the long-term impact of each word you use? You would start to design all of your language just like you set your most important goals. You can use Trigger Words at specific times for precise purposes, and if that's all you do with your words—and if you do it diligently—you'd have enough energy to light up a city. But you can go so much farther! You can use Lifting Words any time of the day or night to fill your language with power and elevate your life to greater heights and happiness. Here are the steps to use Lifting Words in building a life that makes you marvel:

- Make your first word your best word.
- Write a new language with words of power.
- Become a word warrior.
- Test your words and their energy.
- Take action that lifts.

Make Your First Word Your Best Word

"First, verily, are words produced, and the mind runs after them."

— VEDIC PROVERB

There is an old Buddhist saying that shows how necessary it is to immediately lift a thought to a higher experience: *First thought, best thought.* I like to take this idea a step further: *First word, best word.* If it is the first thought that leads to all forthcoming thoughts, then it is the first word that brings forth the next and the next.

The first word is like the engine of a train, pulling all the other words into being. *If you make your first word the best word, it will lead you to the best train of thought.* How many times have you had a negative first word and thought that lead to a whole train of dark and upsetting words and thoughts—ruminations that may have lasted several minutes or even hours?

Well, you are the conductor. And if you stay conscious and diligent, you can change the first word. And that will help you change all the words that follow. So, make *First word, best word* your slogan—in your inner thoughts, in your statements and declarations, and in your conversations with others. Being aware of the first word allows you to create a train of powerful words that will pull your life to superlative success.

First and Best Word Power

Take a moment to experience two very different trains of thought. Close your eyes, and chose one of these words: *bad, horrible, wrong,* or *heavy.* Say it to yourself a couple of times. Then open yourself to the words that naturally come to mind. Notice how the words that follow really carry a hard and heavy feeling, and they may even get worse with each passing word.

Now, take a deep breath, and with your exhalation let all of that go. Begin a new train of thought with one of these as a first word: *best, great, wonderful,* or *happiest.* Repeat the word you choose several times. Then let yourself say the words that spring to mind and follow that energy. Let these *best* words follow one after the other. Notice all of the superlatives that come to mind. Notice, too, how they make you feel.

In this process some people may have heavy words creep into the best, especially if they've had some challenging times. If that happens for you, keep practicing. The wonderful words will start to flow. You can also do this as a word association prayer. Just start with words like *love, holy, spiritual,* or *divine;* and see where they take you.

Write a New Language with Words of Power

Creating a new language requires you to be conscious not only of the negative, limiting words you use, but also of your general language as well. Any and every word can increase or decrease the power, excitement, and vitality you feel. Without going to extremes, you can take some notes in your journal in order to make a study of the words you use in your daily life. Notice the words you use in which places with which people. Writing about the words you use will help you tweak your vocabulary a little bit every day.

Intermittently throughout your day take a moment to tap into the energy and meanings of various random words in your conversations. Just pick one out and feel its energy. This will help you distinguish between the average, daily words that bring you down from the ones that really help you ascend.

Try not to use words that you find meaningless, clichéd, or overused. They are like painting with muddied colors, cutting with a dulled knife, or punching at the wind. At the very least, overused words will be weak and have little power to shape the world you wish to create. At their worst, they'll lessen the energy around them. When you seek to find words with a deeper meaning, you'll find deeper meaning in your life.

Writing the Right Words

When you start to note your replacement words in your journal, you've already begun to write your new story through a changed language. But you can also use your journal to create a list of *empowering* words that you can choose any time to cement your new language. This list acts like a menu that offers you a selection of new exciting words—words that add creativity, enthusiasm, and power to your life every day.

I have a client named Stan who was very busy in his career in corporate management. He was highly motivated to work on changing his words and his life because he thought that his negativity and judgment were at least partly responsible for his recent divorce. (He was right.)

Even though he was committed to working with words, he found that each day would pass without any journal work happening. He just couldn't find the time. I told him to use his journal at bedtime to reflect on his day and the words he used. But during the day he was to take one index card with three to five Lifting Words on one side. He was to use the blank side to write his negative words, then flip the card over to pick a Lifting Word to replace each negative one. He put the word in his breast pocket and used it frequently. It was much easier for him, and he was delighted as he started to feel real changes in his life. Seeing the difference in his outlook, he decided to do other things that would take him deeper in his self-understanding. He enrolled in a meditation class and read many new books. Finding his new self actually became an exciting adventure. And in one of his classes he met someone to share that adventure with him!

So take some words with you in your journal, on a card, or in your smart phone. Even if you can't record the negative words as you use them, replace them immediately with Lifting Words.

Here's a short list that can be a starting point for you. You'll find more Lifting Words in Appendix 1, but be sure, also, to discover your own. You can take a look at your list each morning, and choose one or two words that you can take with you and insert into your language throughout the day.

Some Lifting Words

Joy	Sublime	Brave
Wonder	Lofty	Effective
Uplifting	Gentle	Resilient
Stellar	Noble	Funny
Liberate	Resolve	Peaceful
Persevere	Evoke	Commit
Dazzling	Aware	Yes
Tranquil	Wisdom	Bounty

Incandescent Word Power

Close your eyes. Say to yourself—and feel—the word *incandescent*. Feel that energy completely. Fill yourself with the sparkling light of *incandescence*. In every cell, every thought, every breath, and every moment there is a jubilant, bubbling *incandescent* light.

Whenever you command to yourself *An incandescent life now,* you will be immediately filled with this sparkling, *incandescent* energy. And it will shine onto every step and illuminate every corner of your life.

What a wonderful Power Word *incandescent* is. To think of yourself as *incandescent* is—well—electrifying. And it's so thrilling to lead an *incandescent* life! As you make your roster of empowering and elevating words, realize that the words you use can be unique and special in their meaning and energy, or they can be common and every day. You can give extraordinary and uncommon meaning to common and simple words by creating an emotional engagement with them. You do this by feeling the power and knowing the deeper meaning within each word—even the most basic. With this you can see even the simplest word becomes a word of great power.

Word Power for the Good Life

Feel the word *good* completely. Hold *good* energy inside you. Fill yourself up with *good*. It is the trigger for you to find the goodness in every part of your life. Whenever you say the word *good*, even in passing, you'll focus on the energy of *goodness*.

Every time you say *good morning, good job, good night, good work, good-bye,* you'll remember your intention to truly know *good* then and there. And you'll reach for that deeper meaning—and get it. You'll feel *goodness* in every sense, and others will sense it in you.

Become a Word Warrior

Your language is the arsenal that allows you to wield energy and force in your life. Except for your own spirit, there is nothing of greater power that is more available to you than your words. You can hold yourself in that power and become a Word Warrior just by doing the following:

- **Reach** for the deeper meaning of each word.
- **Engage** with its emotional quality.
- **Be present** in the power and energy of each word.

- **Be fearless** in using words that represent your highest truth possible.

When you approach your new Lifting Words with these actions of mind and heart, even the most common word can help you channel extraordinary energy. Becoming a Word Warrior will give your life deeper meaning, profound purpose, and help you gain ground you never thought possible.

Test Your Words and Their Energy

There are hundreds of words that lift, but since everybody's different, how do you know which word will work best for you? It's simple. All you have to do is close your eyes, and hold the word in your heart, body, and mind. Really breathe deeply, and fill yourself up with it. Sense how you feel and what images come to mind. Be present with the word in every sense.

This test will show you in moments the power that any certain word will hold for you. Try it with any word, and see how you feel. It will fill you up and move through you. But you'd better get started, there are a lot of words to test.

You don't have to do this test with every word, but it's fun to test different kinds of words to see how they feel. Give the words *meatball* or *bowling* a try! But really you want to find the words that lift.

There are words that inspire. There are words that act as a catalyst to higher action and thought. There are some that fill you with hope and excitement, and some that incite more profound contemplation. Words can cause you to seek a higher potential everywhere. It's entirely up to you. Just say the word!

Take Action That Lifts

*"Even if I knew that tomorrow the world would go to pieces,
I would still plant my apple tree."*

— MARTIN LUTHER KING, JR.

When times seem dark, there are actions you can take that generate hope, beauty, and joy. Of course, the first and foremost action you can take is the process of deleting the old negative words and repeating new positive ones. It's important to use your journal and stick with it as long as necessary. You don't change a lifetime habit over night, so it might take a while for your Lifting Words to overtake the limiting ones. But don't give up!

Look at your list of Lifting Words often. Change it regularly. Read it frequently, and choose one or two new words from that list to insert into your language every day. For example, insert the word *happy* or *extraordinary* into your thoughts and conversation as many times as you can today, and see how you feel when you do. Pick a new word every day, put it on a card to take with you, or place it somewhere you can see it to remind you. Mix it up by using common and special Lifting Words—like *joyous* and *incandescent*.

Frequent insertion will insure that you're not only using Lifting Words as a correcting device, but you're also filling your daily language with heightened and joyful energy. All the lifting and empowering words you use will bear fruit in your life over and over again. They will tip the scales in building a critical mass of power and success.

Also, continue to use Trigger Words. These can lead to greater energy and success in specific projects. But more than that, they will complement your work with Lifting Words and significantly accelerate the dynamic shift in your entire language, elevating the energy in your whole life.

There are lots of other lifting actions you can—and must—take that resonate with your extraordinary words. Make another list of the actions you'd like to do to bring growth, well-being, and superlative success, and relationships to your life. This list could include anything—from taking a cooking class or de-cluttering your house, to writing a book or taking piano lessons, to meditating or planning a vacation. Find the actions that will promote your happiness and your truth in power. Then, make sure you take some part of those lifting actions every day. Just like your words, every action that you take is a statement to yourself and to the world.

Time for Results

The results you can gain in working with Lifting Words are enormous—power, joy, a continued state of discovery, and unceasing opportunity. But how long will all of this take? Changing old habits in your language takes time, but the length of that timeline will depend entirely on you. If you take only a few small steps every once in a while, you will stretch out the time it takes. But the more you replace the dark with the light; the more you insert Lifting Words in your language and take the actions that lift; the more you employ Triggering Words for precise purposes—the faster and bigger your results will be. If you hit the ground running every day, the results you seek will occur every day. **Live your life like you *mean* it. Your destiny is in your hands—and in your words!**

Part V

WORDS TO
THE WISE

*"We have only this moment, sparkling like a star
in our hand . . . and melting like a snowflake.
Let us use it before it is too late."*

— MARIE BEYNON

Chapter 19

LACKING—OR
LOOKING FOR—LOVE

*"There is no harvest for the heart alone;
the seed of love must be eternally resown."*

— ANNE MORROW LINDBERGH

There are many people who are looking for a meaningful relationship in their lives. Some are very urgent to do so—indeed a little too urgent. Often, this high level of urgency indicates an inner state of emptiness and a personal definition of lack. This isn't the state of mind that invites opportunity. As a matter of fact, what really occurs is the condition of paradoxical intent, which actually ends up pushing love away. Paradoxical intent is a complex condition, and you can read more about it, and about how to attract the right kind of love in Sandra Taylor's book the *Secrets of Attraction.* For now, let's take a look at the proclamations and declarations our words and actions make about love.

Relationship Declarations

In the realm of relationships, one's words can often contradict one's actions. This makes a very conflicting statement to yourself and to the world. Most people who want a relationship in their lives would probably say, "I want a loving, kind, and reciprocal partner—someone who's really there for me." But their actions may not support this.

Some people live in relationships with partners who are dismissive, rejecting, and uncaring, while others pine for individuals who are unavailable in some way. Both of these groups probably use words like, *I want a happy, reciprocal relationship.* But their actions are declaring quite a different thing. When you stay with someone who's dismissive or when you long for someone who's unavailable, your actions shout to the world, *I want someone who isn't there for me.* Whether a person isn't there actually or isn't there emotionally, *isn't there* is still the operative term.

There's another underlying declaration of lack that is also made by both of these groups. People who stay with or want a person who can't love them are indicating how little they love and honor themselves. They feel like they're empty, so they attract empty people. And the lack of response from the people they attract makes them feel emptier still.

The bottom line is this: emptiness attracts emptiness, and love attracts love. If you want to attract a loving relationship and loving people, you need to be filled to overflowing with love—for yourself, for your life, and for the world. For now, you can begin by understanding a little bit about the nature of love's energy. The more you are filled with your own inner love, the more that message will expand out from you, attracting others who are also filled with love. The emptier you are inside, the more you will attract empty people—people who have nothing to give. What must be done to attract love is to declare your own inner love while simultaneously sending that message to the world.

But how do you create love where emptiness exists? The truth is that love *already* exists; you just don't see it yet. The emptiness is not a real lack; it's a perceived one. Love is a very real and powerful force that exists as a natural part of everyone's spirit. And when it's discovered, get ready for a life of power and joy to be ignited.

"Some day after we have mastered the winds,
the waves, the tides, and gravity,
we shall harness for God the energies of love.
Then for the second time in the history of the world,
man will have discovered fire."

— Teilhard de Chardin

Everyone perceives a sense of lack at some time or another, some people more than others. The experience of lack thrives in the state of victimization. The more victimized one feels, the greater the lack. But there are those who, though they may have been hurt and wounded before, no longer define themselves through it. They now know the great presence and power of love.

The state of lack is a self-deception based on externals. Lack looks outside at what's missing and at what others haven't done for you. Love looks inside at who you are within. Separation from love indicates a perceived separation from one's spirit.

If you have been deeply wounded and have lived for many years with a perception of lack, you will need to pursue this healing in a global way—with many approaches and, perhaps, with the help of teachers or counselors. But whether or not you perceive great lack or just have moments of it now and then, there is a Triggering Phrase that proclaims a tender truth and helps you find the fire of love.

Loving Word Power

Close your eyes and take a moment to simply recall— not relive—a time when you felt a sense of lack. Simply remember it. Now see yourself turning away from that time and that lack. Turn your attention inward. Put your awareness in your heart and feel the warmth of love from your spirit. Take a deep breath and proclaim to yourself, *I am alight with the fire of love.*

Feel the spark of great love ignite within you—glowing and growing and filling you up. It's almost as if you feel fireworks in your heart! You proclaim, *I am alight with the fire of love,* and you feel it. It's a Divine fire, and you are lit with its brilliance.

And you know that in the future, whenever you feel even a moment of lack, you make the proclamation, *I am alight with the fire of love!* And so you are, and so you will be.

I had a client, Roslyn, who had had a very dark and loveless childhood with parents who were very hurtful to her. Her esteem and sense of well-being were virtually nonexistent. When she first started using this *fire of love* process, she said it felt false to her. But she kept it up, and with her meditation, journal work, and counseling, she has become an unbelievably confident, loving, and trusting woman, book editor, wife, and doting mother of two.

Open Heart

Some people may not feel any urgency about romance at all, but would still like a happy relationship. If that's you, there's a command that will help put your heart in a joyful state—open and ready to attract more joyful love back to you. And even if you're not looking for romantic love, it will help you bring love to the whole world and find it in friends and others, as well.

Word Power of the Heart

Close your eyes and take a cleansing, relaxing breath. Send your awareness deep into your heart and begin to feel the great spark of love from your own divine spirit. Feel that pure and tender love stir inside you and start to grow. Say to yourself, *Open, heart!* As soon as you say that gentle command, your heart opens. You feel it open, and you sense the great love that flows through your heart always.

Again you say, *Open, heart!* And your heart opens to the source of eternal love within you. Feel that comfort and support fill you. Decree to yourself, *I don't need to look for love. Love flows through me. Love finds me.* Every time you say the command, *Open, heart!* it acts as a beacon of love to find you, and a beacon of light to the world.

You can say the triggering command *Open, heart!* many times a day. Notice that you're not just saying that you have an open heart. This isn't just a description. You're telling your heart to take action. And when you command your heart to open, it does.

If you have a sense of urgency or lack about love, you should do both of these processes frequently, each time tapping the source of love within you, then sending that love out from you. If the lack is great, you may not feel that inner love strongly at first. That doesn't matter. Do both of these heart processes often any way. They will help remind you of a truth that is everlasting and a love that is, too—even if it feels new to you now.

Regardless if you're looking for romance, both the proclamation and command can help you put greater love into the whole world, sending an embrace to everyone—drycleaners, bank tellers, and others around you. You can lift the energy of love everywhere and bring it back to you from everyone, maybe even from mean bosses and churlish co-workers!

Dealing with the Hard to Love

Sadly, there are too many difficult co-workers and uncivil civil servants. But what do you do when you're confronted by oppositional and intractable people who disrupt your life? Will the command to open your heart change them or the situation? Well, the presence of love may soften their attacks, but their own change must come from within them. Opening your heart during such times will certainly change your perception of the situation. It will help you understand and detach.

Even when dealing with hurtful people, the command, *Open, heart!* will remind you how loving your life experience is, while theirs may be so wanting. It's very easy to feel love for those who are happy and who treat you well. Sending unconditional love to those who are mean-spirited—that's a challenge. Using the *Open, heart!* command reminds you that you have love to spare, even if they don't. It will trigger greater compassion in you, keeping you out of your own anger and the frustration those people cause.

Hurtful people are so entrenched in their egos, they don't consider others' feelings or opinions. If you find these types of people consuming your time and taking center stage in your personal life or at work, it might be time to make the changes that take you out of their reign of terror permanently. That would require serious consideration, courageous action, and some planning. But whether hurtful people play a big part in your life, or you only come across them occasionally, you can still hold love in your heart when they are near. You can also take another step to help yourself—a step back.

The Right Step in Word Power

Imagine that you're dealing with one or two people whom you find intractable and oppositional. The situation requires you to interact with them, and there you are, listening once again to their criticisms, judgments, and negative decrees.

This time you aren't letting it affect you. You take a deep breath and say the command to yourself, *Step back, let go.* And you take a little step back, or you imagine yourself doing so. You tell yourself again, *Step back, let go.* It's an inner command that takes hold. You immediately feel a sensation of stepping away from them and their energy.

Whenever you say the command *Step back, let go,* there's an emotional distance that automatically takes you out of their influence and allows you to detach. You *let go* easily. There's no longer any personal entanglement. And you smile inwardly at the inane posturing you see before you.

This stepping back is something you can practice in any situation where you find yourself dealing with difficult people. You can also use it when you find yourself emotionally invested in other people's responses to you. I taught this technique to a client, Catherine, whose life seemed to be an elevator ride with her son pushing all the up and down buttons. Her son, Michael, was behaving like many teenage boys and being very disrespectful to her. This hurt her deeply because they had been very close all through his childhood and his early teenage years. But now he would often lash out. Even though he would usually come back and apologize to her a day or two later, it did little to relieve the pain.

Catherine was also upset with herself because she would let her son's fickle moods put her in such an emotional tailspin. Then she began using the inner command, *Step back, and let go,* when the conflicts occurred. Every time she did, it helped her get some emotional distance and a broader perspective. Instead of starting a screaming match, she would calmly tell her son that she would talk with him when he could be respectful. Then she would leave the room.

Catherine learned a lesson that lies before everyone. You can't change people, but you can change your responses to them. And that doesn't only mean your outer responses, but your inner responses as well. When you really *step back, and let go,* you won't allow yourself to be put into an adversarial role. You'll be more invested in finding a peaceful outcome for all—and in creating a peaceful state of mind for yourself through simple detachment.

So practice all these loving commands and declarations. They will help you harness the energies of love, discover a new kind of fire, and create peace in your world.

Chapter 20

PLANNING FOR SUCCESS? MAKE YOUR LIFE A VERB

"Action is eloquence."

— WILLIAM SHAKESPEARE

I love the word *promnesia.* It was coined by a psychologist in 1903; and, no, it doesn't mean amnesia of your senior prom— no matter how much you'd like to forget that night! *Promnesia* roughly translates as *memory of the future* and comes from the Greek words *pro* (before) and *mneme* (memory). It can refer to a sensation of remembering something that is occurring for the first time, rather like *déjà vu.* It's also a sense of awareness of what is to come, like *precognition.*

In many ways, we have all seen the future. We have imagined where we are going in life. We have a vision of what lies before us. Our dreams and goals really don't seem to come out of our history, even if they were seeded in the past. Instead, they seem to come out of our future and pull us forward. They compel us to find them and make them real. For me, *promnesia* is the remembering of what we are meant to become.

Word Power in Promnesia

Close your eyes and remember who and what you are to become. Although there may be many roads for you to follow, think of one thing you are compelled to do, one thing you are driven to be. Hold this one thing in your energy fully.

Now, decide on one word or phrase that defines it. How does it feel to hold this as a purpose in your life?

Discovering your purpose is the first step in reaching your goals. Let's take a look at all of the steps that help you realize your goals and dreams:

Steps in Reaching Your Goals

1. Clearly define your purpose.

2. Use words and images of the actions required and the outcomes sought.

3. Change the word *plan* to *approach*.

4. Take action every day.

5. Be present in the process.

6. Be flexible and embrace uncertainty.

7. Recognize every achievement.

8. Understand and release past and present failures.

9. Use words of power, not words of lack.

10. Believe in yourself and in your success.

1. Clearly Define Your Purpose

"Singleness of purpose is one of the chief essentials for success in life, no matter what may be one's aim."

— JOHN D. ROCKEFELLER, JR.

Everybody holds more than one role and one purpose in life. There are career purposes, family purposes, and emotional and spiritual purposes. And even within each one of these, there are many others. You might be a counselor, but you also might teach and write. You may be an actor, but you may also be a dancer, a musician, or a producer.

Singleness of purpose doesn't mean you can't do many things; it means you must do this one thing as a priority, if not every day, most days.

Another element of purpose to be discovered is that of *deeper purpose*. Deeper purpose comes when it is the process itself—the doing it or the being it—that compels you, regardless of the financial or personal gains that may or may not come. Anyone who pursues an action only for the money or fame will soon find that action wanting.

Clearly defining your purpose also requires you to be flexible. Who knows when you may find yourself taken in another direction and shown a new way? Take a few minutes every day to meditate on the purpose that you determined in the promnesia process. Feel its energy, and sense its deepest meaning to you. Assess where that word takes you every day.

2. Use Words and Images of the Actions Required and the Outcomes Sought

Whatever position you want to hold or purpose you embrace, you need to think of it in terms of its action, not just its outcome. Create an image of yourself doing the activity that gets you there.

Action creates your success. And this image will support you in taking that action.

In your mind, never divide an action from its outcome. *Every* action will lead to its natural conclusion. And this must be clear in the words you speak and in the images you visualize. Try also to use the verb of that goal as much as possible, too.

Verb Power

Close your eyes and recall the word or phrase that encapsulates the primary purpose you hold. Determine a verb that best fits that activity.

Take a deep breath. Hold that verb, that word of action, in your mind and heart while you see yourself taking that action. Imagine this clearly and completely for a few moments. Determine a single part of that action you can take today to make that verb real.

Now see the outcome of all the action happily and successfully achieved. Visualize it clearly, almost like a photograph. You have arrived!

I have a client, Jim, who wanted to be a writer. He would subscribe to writing magazines and read books on writers' lives and on how to write. But when I asked what writing project he was doing, he told me that he didn't know what to write. I recommended that he might stop saying, "I am a writer," and start saying, "I am writing," and then take that action every day. First he wrote about his thoughts and feelings. Then he wrote about many of his ideas that came to mind, researching them and discovering more about them. Some of those ideas evolved into published articles. Some are in folders waiting for future projects. Now Jim really is a writer because he actually spends part of every day writing.

3. Change the Word <u>Plan</u> to <u>Approach</u>

*"Where we stand is not as important as the direction
in which we are going."*

— OLIVER WENDELL HOLMES, JR.

I like to use the word *approach* instead of *plan*. Approach feels much more active. Even when you use the word *plan* as a verb, it's only a mental activity at best. Take a moment to notice the difference between these words for yourself.

Approaching Word Power

Close your eyes and say the word *plan*. Bring it into your energy. Don't let your mind go to your own plans. Just feel the word *plan*. You may get an idea of papers, instructions, an outline, or even architectural plans. Hold the word *plan* inside you, and notice that you may feel a little structured or even *rigid*. Also notice that the energy of *should* might come up with the word *plan*.

Now, take a deep breath and let go of that word. Begin to bring into you the word *approach*. Fill yourself with the energy of *approach*. Notice that you almost feel like moving, taking a step, taking action. You may also feel some excitement because you can feel a sense of discovery with the word *approach*.

Of course excising the word *plan* from your vocabulary doesn't mean you have no plan. You have an *approach*, a way to go. It's a vision of the steps that lie before you. You can make a list of the steps, in order to be better organized. In this way you create an *approach* to your purpose. Let yourself feel a sense of discovery with each step, a "coming to meet" with each opportunity. Stay flexible, as the order of things may change, and new ideas may come along. For now, look at your list and simply decide on your first step. Then begin it.

4. Take Action Every Day

> *"Whatever you can do, or dream you can—begin it.*
> *Boldness has genius, power, and magic in it."*
>
> — GOETHE

To achieve success, make your life a verb! Earlier in this chapter you determined what verb would best suit the action of your goal. Well, now that you've got the verb, do the verb. Be the verb! Be aware of all of the verbs—the actions—your goal requires.

Take action and keep taking action every day. Don't wait, but don't be urgent either. Every purpose has its phases. Some phases may be creative and active; some may be receptive and still. Yet, there are actions you can take even during receptive times—contemplation, meditation, trust, receptivity. Open yourself every day to receive insight about the next step. Then take it—staying present with each step along the way.

5. Be Present in the Process

Very much like the goal line in football or the finish line in a race, life's goals are usually seen as something to be reached—to be moved toward or arrived at. This automatically creates a distance between the present moment and the achievement. Striving toward a goal that isn't present almost seems to push it away—removing it from your grasp and requiring you to reach further.

Certainly, when you approach your goals, it is very practical to be aware of the time and phases each step may require. After all, you can't lose 50 pounds by tomorrow or become a best-selling author without writing a book. But in your mind and heart, you can eliminate the distance between you and what you wish to achieve.

All you have to do is create a sense of oneness with your objective and with each step along the way. Be present in each task, and try, also, to cultivate being present with everything in your life. It helps you to fully own each moment and stay open to embrace every opportunity.

6. Be Flexible and Embrace Uncertainty

Flexibility is essential to success. If you adhere too strongly to your agenda you won't stay open to new steps that may lead to a better way.

Word Power of the Unknown

Close your eyes and take a deep breath. There is a specific project or direction you hold in life now. Imagine that project is represented by a path. Imagine yourself looking down that path now.

Realize that somewhere there's another path of great opportunity—one that's going to intersect this path. It's *uncertain* where or how, but it's there. Feel the excitement that there's something unknown, *uncertain* coming. Just beyond, but coming. Oh, happy *uncertainty!*

In order to stay flexible, you not only have to let yourself try new things, you have to seek them out. And sometimes what you might try may not work out. That's okay. Let yourself be wrong.

"Mistakes are portals of discovery."

— James Joyce

Even the things that seem to go wrong can lead to unknown triumphs. So, seek the uncertain, the unseen, the untried. Certainty only closes the door on undiscovered options. When you embrace uncertainty, you embrace the freedom to find new horizons.

7. Recognize Every Achievement

"Whoever I am and whatever I am doing,
some kind of excellence is within my reach."

— JOHN W. GARDNER

Don't wait until you land on distant horizons to recognize the achievements you've made. See achievement in every action you take, whatever the task. Recognize each task as a contribution to your life. If it seems like a mundane and thankless task, thank yourself for completing it. Every step you achieve *is* an achievement. Know it to be so!

There are two things you can do to see achievement in every step toward your purpose. Change the heavy words you associate with your efforts—in any purpose—to words of achievement and contribution. Really feel each endeavor—no matter how small—to be a step toward success and a contribution that you have made toward your dreams.

I have a client, June, who wanted to become a counselor. She needed to get her MSW, but she hated going to school. She found it tedious as well as too limiting in its structure. She called it *an academic straightjacket,* and she procrastinated enrolling in the master's program for months. I told her to try using new words to describe school—*the door to my counseling license,* or *the next step to my success.* She started to use both, and she began to think that way, too. Even when her assignments did become a drudge or when she found the structure of the program limiting, she declared, "This is making a contribution to my life." She was determined to see the accomplishment in each step of the process. And ultimately she accomplished setting up her own private practice, too!

So be sure to see every step as an achievement. And make sure that your sense of achievement spills over into everything you do. Achieve the dishes, accomplish the laundry, achieve your exercise efforts. Even when something in your personal or professional purpose falls short, achieve the new attitude to discover more.

8. Understand and Release Past and Present Failures

Practice nonjudgment—of yourself, of others, of the events in your life. *Take responsibility without taking blame.* Seek to understand the failures you have known, and discover what you can learn from them.

Don't resist acknowledging your mistakes or the obstacles that lie before you. Resistance only wastes your time and keeps you stuck. So seek to find opportunity in obstacles. You might be surprised by what you discover!

"Obstacles . . . can in the long run result in some good end which would not have occurred if it had not been for the obstacle."

— STEVE ALLEN

Always find the benefit in your mistakes—even if the only benefit is knowing what not to do. And no matter what the failure, stay present in your hope and in your power, for both are your greatest resources.

9. Use Words of Power, Not Words of Lack

Saying statements such as, "I don't have enough time," is a pronouncement of lack that you don't want to make true. It's a statement that tells the world you will not succeed until you do have more time. Instead, use the following words: *I take the time I require. The necessary money comes to me. My purpose has duration, and I have the time to realize it.* If you must make an announcement of what you don't have, tell the world that you're without worries. And if you'd like, you can have fun with it, lifting it to higher energy with the French, *sans-souci* ("sahn soo-see")—without worries.

Word Power Without Worry

Close your eyes, take a deep breath, and begin to tap into the strength and harmony that thrive within you. There is a sense of power here. And you make the command, *sans-souci, without worries.* You have every resource at hand, and all the time in the world. *There really are no worries.*

Nothing troubles you now. Everything you need is available to you. And as you take another deep breath, you declare in this perfect state of promise and peace, *There are no worries.*

Continue to be without worries in every part of your life. When you have every resource within you, there really are no worries. Believe it!

10. Believe in Yourself and in Your Success

Belief in yourself is the primary ingredient in any recipe for success. There are plenty of sources for help and guidance in the world, but you are your own expert in your life. Each decision is your own. When you make the choices that honor you and when you take the actions that honor you, pursuing your dreams becomes the natural course of events.

Achieving your dreams also requires your belief in their successful conclusions. The timelines required for success may not be as anticipated. And, in some situations, certain endeavors may not turn out as planned. Belief in your success includes the absolute trust that this or something better shall occur. Know that no matter how things evolve and what events occur, *it's going to happen.*

This is one of my absolute favorite Power Phrases—both in English and in another foreign language: *It sil heve.* It's Dutch, and it's pronounced "It sil haeve." It's fun to say, and it means: *It shall happen* or *It's going to happen.*

Word Power—It's Going to Happen!

Close your eyes and think of a certain purpose that you've been actively pursuing. Hold the idea or specific image of that successful outcome in your mind and heart. Really see it and know it to be so.

Take a deep breath and confidently proclaim to yourself, *It shall happen!* Feel it deeply, surely. Take another deep breath and say again, *It shall happen! It sil heve.* Believe it. Know it. Thrive in it. Delight in it—because *It's going to happen!*

As with all foreign words, be sure to use the English with it for as many days or weeks as it takes for the foreign to carry the same punch of power that the English does. I say this proclamation whenever unfinished or hopeful situations spring to mind. I use it with little things on my schedule, too. When I'm having a busy day, I might wonder if I'll get some time on my treadmill later, I say, *It sil heve.* And somehow, when I say, *It's going to happen,* it does!

Saying that something is *going to happen* doesn't only declare that it will be so, but it also declares that you *trust* it will be so. Trust is the other component to the successful outcome you seek. After you tell the world that *It shall happen,* you have to let it go. Don't worry; don't wonder; don't beg. *Trusting* that *it shall happen* is the very current of energy that this statement carries. If you're questioning all the time and full of doubt, your energy is telling the world that you don't really believe that it's going to happen at all. So, take all the action required, and believe! When you say, *It's going to happen,* see the outcome and know it. Believe it, trust it, and then let it go. Remember . . .

*"Man is so made that whenever anything fires his soul,
impossibilities vanish."*

— LA FONTAINE

Chapter 21

WORDS TO WATCH

"Set a guard, O Lord, over my mouth;
keep watch over the door of my lips."

— PSALMS 141:3

Continue your quest for words that bring you benefit, but also keep a sharp watch for words that can take away. I'm not speaking about those heavy, dolorous words of fear and self-loathing that belong to old, dark histories. We've already talked about ending negative language patterns and building good ones. And that must surely be done. I'm talking about those words that *seem* affirming and strong but carry very different underlying meanings and energies. Let's take a look at some.

Do You Need to Say Need?

I try to keep the word *need* out of my vocabulary—except for the occasional *I need another stapler* or *I need a new frying pan.* And even then I try to say *I will remember to get* a stapler or a frying pan. This option is a command to myself and puts the power in my hands to resolve the issue.

Need is a very easy word to say, and most people probably use it more often than they realize. Even the rich, who have plenty of things, probably fall back on this word a lot. Though this word seems innocuous enough, is it really? Let's find out.

Receiving Word Power

Take a deep breath and bring the word *need* into your-self. Repeat *need, need, need* a few more times. Hold the feeling of *need* deep in your heart and fully inside you. Begin to notice your energy, ideas, and your feelings as you are filled with *need.*

After a few moments, release *need* completely. Take a deep breath, and fill yourself with the word *receive, receive, receive.* Feel *receive* in your mind, your heart, your body. Notice that you may start to feel a sense of readiness. As you say *receive* again, you put yourself in a complete state of *receiving.* You might feel a little excited with the antici-pation of what you are about to *receive.* Notice that in the state of *receiving,* you open yourself to all that the world can bring to you.

Filling yourself with the energy of *need* may have made you feel sad, heavy, or perhaps, empty. You may have even started to think about all of the things that are lacking in your life. But of all the many emotions you might have felt with *need,* it's unlikely that *happy* was one of them. Indeed, here's what *Webster's Diction-ary* tells us about *need:* "lack of something useful; a condition of deficiency; requiring relief; poverty; extreme want; and an urgent requirement of something lacking." That's one boatload of lack and negativity!

And how about the base word for the old European forms of *need?* Well, that base *neu* meant *to collapse with weariness* or *star-vation!* Lovely! I really don't think I want to use the word *need* to describe any part of my life. It's a word that—for centuries upon centuries—has carried the energy and quality of extreme poverty, lack, and want.

And what are the underlying meanings of *need* statements? *I need more money; I need love; I need more time;* all these speak to a grave lack, which you really wouldn't want to be your truth. It might be a great deal better to use: *I make money; I attract love; I find time.* Or, perhaps better still: *Money comes easily; love finds me; time is always available.* You can start to proclaim and command a new truth—a higher truth—rather than *I need, I need, I need.*

It Is Better to Receive than to Need

You can also use the word *receive* for any "needs" you experience and much more. I like to hold the energy of the word *receive* deeply and often in my daily life. You can use any object with this verb—I *receive* love, wealth, help . . . anything. I often put no object after this beautiful verb and simply hold myself in a deep state of *receiving,* as we had done in the previous process.

Doing this can put you in an open type of *receiving.* It is a wonderful, unpredictable, and happy state of being. You'll find yourself filled with the excitement of something coming—some unknown gift just around the corner.

I shared this process with a friend, Julie, who—like me—is a big fan of stage and theatrical musicals. She began inserting the word *receive* into her heart and mind throughout her day. She said that, after a while, holding the energy and meaning of the word *receive* started to take her immediately back to the play *The Music Man.* The scene where the Wells Fargo Wagon comes down the street to make a delivery would spring to her mind. If you've seen the play or movie, you'd remember that scene where the whole town lines the street, in rapt excitement, anticipation, and expectancy. There's going to be a delivery of some wonderful, unknown package for some lucky unknown person. Julie told me that when she holds the word *receive* now, her energy lifts immediately. She starts looking through her day for a Wells Fargo Wagon full of unexpected gifts. On many days there would be surprises of assistance, joyful moments and even gifts from her boyfriend! Even just her lift in mood was a present she gave herself. How much happier her life became when she would ask herself, *What special something could be coming today?*

Receiving is a state of promise, mystery, and wonder. *Need* proclaims lack. *Receive* answers, "Maybe it's not here yet—but something's coming around the corner. Just you wait and see!"

Protection or Power?

Which would you prefer, protection or power? Is it really either one or the other? Indeed it is. Needing protection and knowing your power are mutually exclusive events. You can't be vulnerable and powerful at the same time, just as you can't be pregnant and not pregnant at the same time.

There is a great trend in the world today for people to believe they need protection—protection from negative people, places, thoughts, and even spirits. At the same time, many people believe they have a boundless power to manifest the reality they seek. But which is it? Are you vulnerable or powerful? My money's on the latter! As a mater of fact, I rarely use the word *protection* except to teach people not to use the word *protection*. It's just one of those words that seems promising but lies to you about who you are and about the power you have.

Word: *Power*

Close your eyes and take a deep breath. Bring into your experience the words *I need protection.* Fill yourself with the *need for protection. Needing protection* sends other statements to the universe: *I'm vulnerable. I'm afraid.* Notice how *needing protection* feels. You may feel like hiding or taking cover. Perhaps you're feeling weak, or even helpless.

Now take another deep breath and release the energy of *needing protection.* Send it all away from you. Align yourself with your eternal reality. And with your next breath, bring the words *boundless power* into your mind, your heart, your body. Feel the energy of *eternal, divine power* and really fill yourself with it. Repeat *boundless power* several times, and notice how you feel and what you feel, in every part of you.

It's not hard to see that, when somebody says, "I need protection," the underlying statements are *I'm vulnerable, I'm afraid,* and *I need someone else to take care of me.* It's an entirely different energy when you define yourself through the word *power.* Expressing surety in your *strength* tells the world you approach life with confidence and even fearlessness. It's a good feeling to have.

Don't get me wrong. I'm not suggesting reckless behavior. It would still be a bad idea to buy property near Chernobyl, smoke three packs of cigarettes a day, or take leisurely walks through the worst part of town at midnight wearing your diamonds. Powerful is not the same as stupid.

The bottom line is this: Your words make up your thoughts and energy. And your thoughts and actions create your life. Having a poverty mentality supports continued poverty. Believing you are vulnerable and need protection supports continued vulnerability and helplessness. Any word you use invokes the exact energy of that word from a very responsive world around you. Would you really want to attract people and situations that prove you are vulnerable?

This is not just a matter of semantics; it's a matter of energy. It's a matter of definition. When you define yourself as vulnerable, needing protection, it says that you are also defining yourself from only a vulnerable, and personal, worldview. But when you define who you are beyond that narrow temporal perspective, you declare that you know your power—your real, unimpeachable power.

Just as Power Words are an interior language, the real power in your life is an interior—yet inexhaustible—power. Know it! And if you don't know it yet, use the words that convince you.

When you use the word *power,* know your *power to be boundless.* When you use the word *strength,* know it to be *limitless.*

"The high strength of men knows no content with limitation."

— AESCHYLUS

Abundant Heart, Abundant Life

We should try to be precise with every word we use, and certainly that includes Power Words and declarations. If you want to proclaim your financial prosperity, then it's best to use words such as *wealth, prosperity, financial abundance,* or others that you'll find with the Prosperity Power Words in Chapter 6. Still, there are many financially rich people who would say they are poor in too many ways. It's so important to proclaim your abundance of every stripe—spiritual, personal, creative, and financial. A truly rich life has many layers. And I like to embrace and be thankful for all of them—for *full abundance.* For this I like to use the Manx Gaelic Power Words *lane palchis* (pronounced "len pahl-chis"). It means *full abundance,* and it speaks to a life that's bountiful in every corner.

Abundance in Every Way

Take a moment to think about all the ways your life is abundant. Hold that richness in your heart for a moment. Now, close your eyes and take a deep breath. Begin to open yourself to your *abundant spirit*—that part of you that knows no want, no lack, and only *abundant love and power.* Feel that fill you absolutely.

Relax more deeply, and hold the words *abundant time and immeasurable joy* inside you. Feel yourself filled and surrounded by the energy and ease of this boundlessness. Say the words *lane palchis* and embrace the *full and timeless abundance* that never wanes. It fills every part of your life and every experience you have. Notice how you feel as you take another deep breath in your *full abundance* and say, *thank you.*

Always be sure to see and appreciate all of the ways you already have *abundance* in your life. Knowing the truth of your *abundance* in all ways—personal, creative, spiritual, and financial—supports your further abundance everywhere. To always define yourself as bountiful creates a reality of unceasing bounty in every part of your life.

And make sure you feel abundant gratitude as well. There's nothing so happy as truly knowing where your happiness lies—inside you where no lack exists.

> *"Giving thanks for abundance is sweeter than*
> *the abundance itself."*
>
> — R U M I

Which Words Work?

Plenty of new words are going to come along in your life. As a matter of fact, using Power Words effectively requires you to find and use new words regularly.

Some words seem beneficial, but they can really take you another way. Some words work great for other people, but they may not move you. How can you really tell if any particular word works as a Power Word for you? If you're not sure, here are a few easy steps to let you know.

Steps in Determining Effective Power Words

1. Ask yourself, *What is the underlying statement—the hidden message—that this word is giving to me and to the world?* Be aware not only of the word's deeper meanings, but also of its connotations. If the underlying statement is something you wouldn't like to make true, don't use the word. If the word doesn't seem as precise as it could be, find another.

2. Always spend a few minutes to deeply feel the energy of the word. Bring it inside you, as we've been doing throughout this book. Take a deep breath, and feel every nuance, and sense any image

or idea that comes to mind—and be sure to *trust* what you feel and sense about the word completely.

3. Once you find a word with the right underlying meaning and good energy, start to put that word to work. Use the word as a Power Word, and insert it into your life often. Apply it to the situations where its energy can be helpful. See what emotional, mental, and physical actions that it immediately triggers for you. If it has the impact you want, it's the right Power Word for you.

Can You Say Wonderful?

There is another question you can ask when you're trying to determine if any specific word should be in your vocabulary. It's something I use myself, and it comes from the Latin *Mirabile dictu* ("mee-ráh-bee-lay dik-too"). Is it *wonderful to say?*

Word Power of Wonder

Close your eyes, and think of any word that you already use or wonder about using. Hold it in your mind. Think about what it really means to you.

Then move your focus out of your head and into your body and feelings. Repeat the word, taking it deeply inside you, and notice everything you sense. Pay attention especially to the feelings and responses it triggers. What does it make you want to think or do? See the action this word would trigger. Is it action that you would want to take?

Now, let all of that go. Take a deep breath, and say the word again. Ask yourself, *Is this word Mirabile dictu? Wonderful to say? Does it feel marvelous to use?* If it does, then use it with power, and purpose, and happiness.

Be Vigilant, Not Militant

"I will speak excellent and princely things;
and the opening of my lips shall be for the right thing."

— PROVERBS 8:6

Stay ever vigilant in using your words. Try to be precise, and deeply experience your words. Clearly, even words that seem fine can have other subtle meanings that make you feel very vulnerable or disempowered.

When you use a negative word, don't make yourself wrong. Make yourself learn. Make yourself love. And make yourself do it over. Certainly, don't treat yourself harshly when you end up using a depleting or negative word. You don't have to become the grand inquisitor or even the word police. There will be times that you fall back into old patterns, but you don't have to make yourself wrong. Unkindness to self and to others is the most unfortunate thing anyone can do with words.

If you have a slip of the tongue or mind, and you use a word that you're trying to excise from your language, respond with *ease* and *forgiveness*. Take a deep breath, and bring the words *ease* and *forgiveness* into you, holding them in your heart and feeling them deeply. Forgiving—and loving—yourself is a far better way to go than making yourself wrong.

Pat yourself on the back, too, because you're living so consciously that you were aware of the slip. Treat yourself kindly, and be proud of the work you do with words. Each and every word can be a blessing in your life.

Chapter 22

THE LAST WORD

"There are only two ways to live your life.
One is as though nothing is a miracle.
The other is as though everything is a miracle."

— ALBERT EINSTEIN

Determine now that every word you use will take you farther. Begin to *command* your unlimited power, *proclaim* your profound love, and *trigger* the brilliant truth you are. You can make every moment of every day another sublime miracle in an exalted and glorious life of miracles. And your words can help you do it.

I'd like to share just a few more Trigger Words that can help spark your connection to the unending inner fire that creates all miracles in your life. It's lightning that you won't just capture in a bottle; you'll capture in you!

Lightning Word Power

Close your eyes, and take a deep breath. As you draw your focus deeper and deeper inside you, start to feel the great electrical force and power that sparks within you. Say to yourself *lightning force,* and really take a moment to feel this dynamic, *lightning power* deep inside you.

This power seems to grow and spark and flash as you continue to hold the words *lightning force.* You feel empowered to do anything, and you are determined to strike out in new directions. You feel a *lightning power* inside you, and with it you are ready to act, to be, to do—without a moment's hesitation.

You can tap this *lighting force* anytime throughout your daily life—anytime that you want to feel and express your deepest inner power. You can use it whenever you're not feeling confident or strong, or whenever you're feeling disconnected from that spirit inside you. This lighting force is your natural inner power, and all you have to do is go within to tap it.

Looking Inside with Words

"Who looks outside dreams; who looks inside wakes."

— C.G. JUNG

There is nothing more key to finding that spirit within you and capturing that inner lightning than the practice of meditating. To tap that great electrical force, you simply have to plug in.

You can combine your self-awareness with your word awareness by bringing one or two Power Words to your meditations. It can be any word you'd like, any word that lifts your life and purpose. Just spend a few minutes holding the word and its concept in your heart and mind. You don't have to say the word over and over. Just repeat it now and again while you fill yourself with the experience of its energy, feeling, and purpose.

As you feel and hold that energy, determine to insert that word into your language throughout your day, whenever the opportunity allows. Take it with you on a card as a reminder. Insert it when you're thinking, insert it when you're speaking. Every time you hear it, think it, speak it, or use it in any way, be sure to take just a moment or two to feel its energy. And when you feel that energy, also send it out from you and into the world. It only takes a minute to *know* the energy that you're putting into you and putting out to others. Over time, be sure to vary the words you insert into your life. When you truly know the power of each word you use, you can recognize the contribution you're making to the world.

What Happens Now?

> *"Light tomorrow with today."*
>
> — ELIZABETH BARRETT BROWNING

Today is the day you make your future. Your new thoughts today become the foundation of future belief and future realities. New disciplines can become tried and true habits. And distant horizons can be closer than you think. Tomorrow's worth is founded in today's. And today's worth is funded by you.

I had a client named Roger who tended to be a big worrier—about work, about his family, about everything. I taught him the following commands to help move him out of his worries and put him squarely in the immediate moment. He not only left his worries behind, but he found a new excitement and energy with his family and with his life that he never thought existed. He once told me, "These words brought me a sense of discovery about every moment! I treasure everything so much more than I used to."

Life is filled with a million little moments that seem to hardly matter at all, but each moment is the building block of tomorrow. It's possible for you to fill each of life's moments with depth and meaning.

Word Power Now

Close your eyes and take a deep breath. Say to yourself, *Meaning now.* And as soon as you connect with the command, *meaning now,* you look for—and discover—some *meaning* in this moment *now.*

Let that go, and with another deep breath, say to yourself, *Value now.* As soon as you say *value now,* you find some *value* in this very moment. And if the apparent *value* in this moment eludes you, you acknowledge a value in you.

Releasing that, you then say the words, *Depth now.* And immediately you go inward to the very *depth* of your being, The *depth* of your soul. And there, too, you find *meaning.* And there, too, you find *value.* And there, too, it is always *Now.*

Like Roger, I use these quick and easy—yet profoundly effective—commands throughout my day. And they have quite literally brought richness to my life that's hard to describe. It's a richness that is seized moment by moment, *and found in the most unlikely places.*

You can use these commands in any situation and with any person. You can find the *meaning, value,* and *depth* everywhere. But you have to capture it *now.* Of course, you can say an affirmation like, *I'm able to find the meaning in this situation.* But when you say the command, *Meaning now,* your response is not just analytical, it's visceral and immediate.

If there is power in finding the *meaning, value,* and *depth* in life, how much more power would there be in doing that every possible moment that you can? Don't wait until tomorrow to discover meaning, know your value, and experience depth. Do it *now!*

The Best Word

Compassion may be the greatest contribution that anyone could make to the world. Its benefit is measureless. And when you use it as a Power Word, holding it deep inside you, the change it makes in you—and in the world—is measureless, too.

You can do the following process anytime words of judgment and intolerance—whether for yourself or others—creep into your inner or outer language. And remember, you have not cultivated real success until you have cultivated compassion.

Compassionate Word Power

Close your eyes, and take a deep breath. Bring the word *compassion* deep inside you. Fill yourself with the energies of this beautiful word.

It's almost as if you hear an inner whisper: *compassion.* And you feel yourself fill with *softness, sympathy,* and *kindness.* Take another deep breath, and again say *compassion.* Notice that you are wrapped in *gentleness* and *peace.* You're filled with a *deeper understanding* and a *loving wisdom.* With another deep breath, feel *compassion* stir inside you. Then send it forth.

Compassion is a big word for me. And although some Trigger Words can lose their impact with frequent use, *compassion* has never lost its power for me. You can use *charity, kindness, tolerance,* or any other compassionate quality if you'd like an alternative. You can also use the Tibetan word for *compassion: karuna,* or another language if you'd like. It really doesn't matter which word you'd like to use, as long you use it. Intolerance for others breeds it in the self. Compassion bred is compassion held for all.

So become a source of compassion in the world—both to yourself and to others. There's too much pain and too little understanding already. When you share *compassion, charity,* and *gentleness,* you teach *compassion, charity,* and *gentleness.* When you meet a person who sees the glass as half empty, fill it. When you hear an intolerant word spoken by another, take a moment to change it in your mind. Mentally send the good and kind word back to that person. When you see good in a person or situation, acknowledge it. Speak about it to that person. Any act of *compassion* brings *charity* and *gentleness* to the world. What kind of world could it be, if everyone's first response and action were *compassion?*

Much More Beyond

"The most beautiful thing we can experience is the mystery."

— ALBERT EINSTEIN

There are so many wonderful words and phrases that I use so often, sometimes I feel like each of them is my favorite. A number of Power Words are pinned to my bulletin board, but there's only one on a glazed plaque on my wall: *Plus ultra.* It's Latin, and it means *More beyond.* In ancient times *plus ultra* was written on maps to indicate the unknown areas where no one had yet gone—the very edges of the world.

In those days, it was a hopeful and, perhaps, cautionary title. After all, if you go too far, you might find more. Or you might fall off!

Plus ultra means quite a different thing now—indeed, so many liberating things! It means there's *more beyond* in every part of your life. There's more *beyond* this time, if time feels lost to you. There's more beyond this place, if this place feels wrong to you. There's more beyond these people, if they disappoint you. And there's more beyond this physical world, if it limits you.

Plus ultra can take you out of the disappointments of this mundane world. But even more than that, it fills you with the wonder of what is *beyond* this mundane world. *More beyond* takes you out of the personal and into a larger unlimited reality.

Word Power Beyond

Close your eyes and declare to yourself, *There's more beyond.* Begin to feel the great expansive energy of *more beyond. Beyond the next corner there are more possibilities. Beyond this moment there are more opportunities.* Take a moment to really feel the excitement and mystery of what lies *beyond.*

Now take a deep breath, and again say *Plus Ultra, more beyond*. Within you, you become aware of a larger reality *beyond* the personal, a timelessness *beyond* time, and a Self *beyond* self. You expand, and your own energy expands, and with another breath you say *Plus Ultra*.

The Power Phrase *more beyond* is filled with undiscovered opportunity and catch-your-breath wonder. With it, you know that you can see beyond, know beyond, and go beyond expected boundaries and into new worlds. There are few words that carry an energy of greater promise than *plus ultra* or *more beyond*. But let's explore a surprisingly common word that can.

The Last Word Is the Next Step

I love the word *become* because of the enormous potential it carries. I use it here as the last word because it is the stepping-stone to each new word—and to each new world to come.

There are a few different ways to use the word *become* as a Power Word. Sometimes, I teach my clients to simply say, "I become _____," leaving a space to invite the first word that comes to mind—a word that shows them what they could *become* that moment, that hour, that day.

Often their answers would be very simple ones—*good, wise, strong, forgiving, happy,* and *diligent* are just a few. Inevitably, the answer that would fill in the blank would always be a certain fit for what's happening for them that day.

I remember one client, Richard, who was a businessman with a stubborn streak and a rigidly scheduled life. When he did this little process, he got the same spontaneous response many days in a row: *I become flexible*. What he actually became was very frustrated. I told him that he kept getting the same response over and over because he actually *had* to *become more flexible*—not just think about it. He had to catch himself when he started controlling or posturing. And slowly he actually did. He started to become more adaptable and spontaneous—listening more, letting go of control, altering his schedule, and adding more things and people he enjoyed. He was not only much happier, but he also became more socially and physically active. He started exercising, and even his rheumatoid arthritis pain eased. Talk about flexible!

Of course, for all those who ask what they should *become,* getting the answer isn't the point. *Becoming* the answer is the point! It's not enough just to think about what you could be. It must be felt. It must be done. Whatever you are meant to *become, become* it!

Becoming Word Power

Close your eyes, and say to yourself, *I become . . .* and open yourself to the first word that follows. Be spontaneous. Say, *I become . . .* and perceive the first word immediately. Make yourself get a word—the first word that comes to mind.

Don't start analyzing why you got this word; just take it into your body and heart. *Become* it fully for a few minutes, holding this word deep inside you. *Become* it in energy, in body, in action. See the steps that you can take to support this *becoming.* Notice everything. Declare this *becoming,* and know that it is so.

Getting the answer to *I become* and then *becoming* the answer is a wonderful technique that you can use anytime throughout your day. I do this often. I like the idea of having a new *becoming* in any moment.

A Greater Becoming

I also use this very powerful Power Word in little meditations that I call sacred moments. Only this time, I don't fill in the blank with any particulars. I simply open to the state of *blissful becoming.*

Unsurpassed Word Power

Close your eyes and say to yourself, *I become,* without following it with any specific word. If a describing word pops into your mind, take a deep breath and send it away. Again gently say, *I become* with no word after it. Notice that you're not limited by even the most expansive word. You're not limited by any word at all.

Hold the energy of an *unsurpassed becoming* inside you. Say *I become* again, and notice that you start to feel an unlimited potential and possibilities. You might even feel like you're expanding out to the stars. In any moment you can *become* who you have been forever. Hold deep inside you the grandness, joy, and unbounded reality that this word, *becoming,* gives you. Feel this *becoming* in every part of you, and know that each new day is an invitation to *become.*

I have a client, Nora, whose past was so turbulent and dark that she had considerable trouble defining herself in any other way. Stuck in a dead-end job, she was shy and self-dismissive. And she desperately needed to see herself in a new way. I suggested that she use both of the *becoming* processes several times a day. With the first, she was to follow the declaration *I become* with any strong purpose, action, or self-description. Then immediately after that, she would take a moment to experience her greater *becoming*—a *becoming* beyond her personal self. Over time, her perception of herself began to change from her limited and past defeats to her present—and, indeed, eternal—potential. She has taken back her confidence and power. She lives a joyful life and has created a great career helping people in love. She is a well-noted wedding planner who is so popular that she has a two-year waiting list.

This inner, unlimited *becoming* takes you to your spiritual fire inside. Go there! The more you do, the greater you will *become!*

Becoming really does create a sacred moment, but there are hundreds of Power Words—in this book and those you find for yourself—that can help you make each moment sacred. And there are many more Trigger Words that can help you realize every success and joy, too. But you must speak like you mean it. You must choose your words well. Use your interior experience of each word—its energy, feeling, deeper meaning, and force. This inner pursuit is what will give you the power in Power Words. And be sure to use your interior self in *all* things. It will set apart an average life from an extraordinary life.

Discovering Fire

> *"The mind is a tool, a machine moved by spiritual fire."*
>
> — FYODOR DOSTOYEVSKY

Many people—and perhaps all people at some time in their lives—ask, *What's the point?* And I think the ultimate point is the same for each of us—whether you're a poet, an architect, a teacher, a mom, a bus driver, or a maintenance man. The point for everyone is to find that spiritual fire within—and be lit by it.

Finding your spiritual fire is inevitable if you keep looking within. It's impossible if you don't. But Power Words can help you. They allow you to use your language—and your focus—to go within and bring that inner fire out. They lift your energy, and they trigger the results that light up your life.

So use your words of power, and let yourself be lit by them. *Go* within. *Choose* within. *Think* within. And *be* within. And you *will* discover fire.

AFTER WORDS

You've seen how significantly a variety of different words can impact you, but there are a few more practices that you might want to add to your word bag of tricks that can come in handy throughout your day. Let's take a look.

Opposites React

There is a Latin saying from ancient times called *Tactica Adversa*. It means *Adverse Tactic* or *Opposite Approach*. Genghis Khan used this practice in his battles during which his men would feign retreat so that his enemies would pursue them. Then his forces would turn and attack. Though the term *Tactica Adversa* goes back to ancient Rome, more than a thousand years before Khan's time, this *Opposite Approach* is still an effective life strategy when you apply it to your actions and words.

It's very simple really. Whenever you find yourself engaged in a destructive or sabotaging behavior, you immediately change it to an opposite action. And whenever you find yourself using negative or defeating words—whether about yourself or another—you change them to their opposites.

Sometimes, if you're feeling down, these new opposite and beneficial words may feel false to you at first. But recognize that these new words actually describe a new experience, a greater potential, and a higher truth—your higher truth. You can use this *Opposite Approach* any time a destructive word comes to mind or mouth. Here are some examples for you.

Opposite Approach

worry — trust
down — up
hopeless — hope-filled
tired — energized
heavy — light
wounded — healed
empty — filled

These are just a few ideas. You can take any difficult, dark word and turn it to its opposite any time. Give it a try. You may find that opposite words can lead to quite a different life.

Verbal Action

Earlier we looked at the effect of bringing Power Words to your actions. But there are also a few ways that you can bring action to your Power Words. When you use words such as *freedom, power, joy,* or any other Power Word, hold each one deeply inside you as you've already learned. Then let yourself get a sense of the *action* of that word. Just imagine how a word such as *freedom, power,* or *joy* would feel as a *verb.* Then ask yourself what each of these words would move you to do. You'll find that by turning a *being* word into an *action,* you can put a great deal of momentum into your life and power into your dreams. Here's an example.

The Act of Being

Close your eyes, and take a deep breath. Fill yourself with the word *freedom.* As you sense the energy of *freedom* filling you up, let yourself also feel *movement and stirring* of this energy inside you. Take a moment to really feel the action of *freedom* now.

Now let all of that go. And with your next deep breath, bring in the word *power*. Fill yourself with the feeling, energy, and *stirring of power*. Feel *power's action* within you. How does *power move* you?

Take another deep breath, and with your exhalation, let that go. Begin to bring inside you the word *joy*. With every passing moment you can sense *joy* filling you up, but it is more than just a filling. It's a *swirling, bubbling action of joy!* Take a moment to feel how *joy* moves you.

After you sense this completely, take another deep breath and relax further. Take a moment to determine one act of *freedom*, one act of *power*, and one act of *joy* that you can do today. Really think about this now. Decide the steps that you can take to act on your *freedom*, your *power*, your *joy*. Make a commitment to take these actions. And realize that when you bring *action* to *being*, your *being* becomes powerful.

Seize More Than the Day

Carpe Diem, or *Seize the day,* is one of the world's great inspirational commands. It directs you to grab the moment, to put it in hand, and to embrace and use it right now.

I love to let old words inspire new words—combining different Power Words and putting little twists on old-time declarations and sayings. *Seize the day* is one command that I like to tweak for a whole new meaning. Imagine that command changed by just one word: *Carpe Deus, Seize the divine.*

Carpe Deus

Relax for a moment and take a deep breath. Begin to think of who and what God is to you. Close your eyes, and with your next deep breath bring the word *divine* inside you. Feel the qualities of *divine love, divine power,* and *divine peace* fill you. Whenever you bring the *divine* into you, this overwhelming embrace of *eternal power, unlimited love,* and *absolute peace* are yours completely. Take a moment to feel this and anchor this *divine* experience in your reality now.

There are times throughout your day when you may feel nervous, angry, confused, hurt, or doubtful. When this happens, it's important to bring back the feeling and memory of your *divine* reality into your awareness. At these times, all you have to do is take a deep breath and say the command, *Seize the divine. Carpe Deus.* And with that command, you will immediately recall that *divine* reality and bring *divine love and power* within.

Say *Seize the divine* to yourself again now, and feel yourself fill up with *divine grace and power.* Whenever you say *Seize the divine* in the future, this feeling is renewed. With this command you see every situation and every person from *an eternal perspective, a divine understanding,* and *a perfect peace.* Whenever you say the words *Seize the divine,* you do.

This wonderful command is a frequent one for me. Of course there are quiet moments, such as during meditation or just contemplative thought, where my experience of the *divine* is a gentler embrace and becoming. Still, there are challenging times during the day when you just have to make a quick grab for that *divine understanding and peace* before it gets away from you. That's when I use this command most.

Divine may be the most powerful of all Power Words. With that energy within, you can bring *divine power and love* to every and any moment. So, regardless of whether you *seize the divine* or *embrace the divine,* the operative word here is *divine.* Become it every day!

APPENDIX 1:
LIFTING WORDS

Here are some Lifting Words for you to plant in your daily experience. Put some on cards and take them with you, using them frequently. When you use them and open your heart to the depth of their meaning and force, they can lift the power of your life the very moment you reach for their energy.

Magnify	Free	Delight
Elevate	Peace	Uphold
Lift	Love	Bright
Expand	Excite	Reflect
Advance	Glowing	Reach
Increase	Brilliant	Shine
Liberate	Luminous	Transform
Prevail	Kind	Abide
Triumph	Splendor	Radiant
Endure	Sparkling	Extraordinary
Calm	Duration	Renew
Broaden	Gentle	Aspire

APPENDIX 2:
THE ENERGY OF COLORS

Some people experience a sense of color when they focus on the energy of words. These color experiences may mean different things for different people, but there are also universal meanings to the colors as shown below. If you sense colors in word energy, give yourself time to see how those colors feel and what they mean to you. You are unique. Trust what happens for you.

Color	Key Words
Red	Speed, heat, power, energy, action; sometimes conflict
Orange	Vitality, regeneration, warmth, logic, science, detail
Yellow	Healing, philosophy, intellect, creativity, joy
Green	Balance, peace, healing, expansion, abundance, growth
Pink (and Burgundy)	Love, marriage, family, devotion, release of conflict
Blue (and Indigo)	Communication, spirituality, intuition, psychism, clairvoyance, calm, unconditional love
Violet/Purple	Spiritual unfoldment, transformation, discipline, mysticism, rituals, leadership
Black	Meditation, structure, lessons, duty, karma, restriction
Brown	Reliability, stability, grounding, detail, follow-through, science; sometimes stubbornness
Milky White or Silver	Reflection, motherhood, emotions, receptivity, intuition
Clear (or Brilliant White)	Purity, clarity, spiritual power, selflessness, higher purpose, penetrating thought

APPENDIX 3:
WORDS OF BLESSING

Here are some alternatives for *Bless you*. You can also look into more languages for alternatives that strike your fancy.

- *God bless you*
- *Blessings to you*
- *Blessed be*
- *Blessings forever*
- *Blessings to all*
- *Bendiciones* (Spanish)
- *Gesundheit* (German)
- *Bénédictions* (French)
- *Na Zdravje* (Slovenian)
- *Gezondheid* (Dutch)

ACKNOWLEDGMENTS

My deepest appreciation and gratitude go to the following extraordinary people:

Those who helped me with this book in so many ways: Lisa Bernier; Ed Coughanor; Barbara, Joanna, and Mary van Rensselaer; Ben Gleisser; Tammy Hildreth; Ros Burton; Rhonda Lamvermeyer; Devin Staurbringer; and—most of all—to my twin sister, Sandra Anne Taylor, whose care and help in all things have always been invaluable. My gratitude and love are beyond measure.

My wonderful family: Devin Staurbringer, my dear son, and his kindred spirit, Kayla Cwalinski; Sarah Marie Klingler, my devoted, loving mother; my sister, Sandra, and her husband and family, Benjamin, Vica, Jenya, Ethan, and Yvonne Taylor; and my other son, Dr. Jeremiah Freedman, and his wife and children, Deanna, Isaac, and Molly. And to the rest of my family of home and heart: Kevin and Kathryn Klingler; Marilyn, Emily, James, and Rick Verbus; Linda Smigel; Rosie and Carol Staubringer; and Carmine and Marie Romano.

My colleagues and friends: Tom and Ellie Cratsley; Dr. Neal Rzepkowski; Donna Eden and David Feinstein; Valerie Darville; Julianne Stein; John C. White; Loren Schuh; Dr. George Berki; Graeme Lloyd; Bryan James; B. Anne Gehman and Dr. Wayne Knoll; Lucinda Wilson; Cindy Kaza; Adam Bernstein; Tom Bundy; Michael Freedman; John Holland; Peggy Rometo; Darren Weissman; Lisa Williams; Joanne and Jaccolin Franchina; Rose Vanden Eynden; Victor Paruta; Mary McCann; Cinnamon Mancini; Gloria Weichand; Mark Abushady and Ken Mathis; Danielle Lang; Shelly and Frank Takei; Lou Ann Beecher and the folks at Serenity; Amy Gary; James Pell; Joseph Tittel; Dee Wallace; Jessie Furst; Janice

Dreshman; Brecht and Sara Saelens; Dan Johnson and Tom Elkas; and George Koury.

To those whose superlative efforts have made my work easier: Lucy Dunlap, Andrea Loushine, Cheri Polk, Emily Manning, Michelle Smith, Faith and Danielle Miller, Caroline Newbury, Paul Zegarac, and Jason Carnes.

To every community around me: Sue, Joanne, and all my wonderful friends in Lily Dale; to Barbara Sanson, Carolyn Sampson, and all those who serve at the Healing Temple; to Jane Gibson, Jean, and all the exceptional people at BrightLife, The Isle of Man; to everyone who brings so much light and joy to me wherever I teach around the world—my students, clients, group members, and my audiences everywhere—you have all meant so much to me. You will never know how deeply you have touched my life. And to all those unseen but never unappreciated. I stand on the shoulders of your strength and inspiration!

About the Author

Sharon Anne Klingler, an inspiring international speaker and author, is the best-selling co-author of *Secrets of Success* with Sandra Anne Taylor and the author of *Intuition & Beyond,* as well as many other titles. One of the world's leading intuitives, Sharon has been featured on major television outlets, including the Oprah Winfrey Network; the Discovery Channel; BBC and ITV London; BBC Scotland; VTV Canada; NBC, ABC, and CBS affiliates; and on major outlets throughout Australia, Europe, and the United States. She has also appeared in magazines and newspapers in London, Sydney, Melbourne, New York, and across the United States.

Sharon maintains a private practice with high-profile clients from around the world. She lectures at some of the world's leading conferences and centers for learning, including Georgetown University in Washington, D.C., Alternatives–St. James's Church in London, and the Lily Dale Assembly in New York, among many others throughout the U.S., Europe, Canada, New Zealand, and Australia.

Find out about Sharon's CDs and other titles at www.Sharon AnneKlingler.com.

Hay House Titles of Related Interest

YOU CAN HEAL YOUR LIFE, the movie, **starring Louise Hay & Friends**
(available as a 1-DVD program and an expanded 2-DVD set)
Watch the trailer at: www.LouiseHayMovie.com

THE SHIFT, the movie,
starring Dr. Wayne W. Dyer
(available as a 1-DVD program and an expanded 2-DVD set)
Watch the trailer at: www.DyerMovie.com

*SECRETS OF ATTRACTION: The Universal Laws of Love, Sex,
and Romance,* by Sandra Anne Taylor

MESSAGES FROM WATER AND THE UNIVERSE, by Masaru Emoto

QUANTUM SUCCESS: The Astounding Science of Wealth and Happiness,
by Sandra Anne Taylor

EXPERIENCE YOUR GOOD NOW! Learning to Use Affirmations,
by Louise L. Hay

TUNE IN: Let Your Intuition Guide You to Fulfillment and Flow,
by Sonia Choquette

*SECRETS OF MEDITATION: A Practical Guide to Inner Peace
and Personal Transformation,* by davidji

WISHES FULFILLED: Mastering the Art of Manifesting,
by Dr. Wayne W. Dyer

All of the above are available at your local bookstore,
or may be ordered by contacting Hay House (see next page).

We hope you enjoyed this Hay House book. If you'd like to receive our online catalog featuring additional information on Hay House books and products, or if you'd like to find out more about the Hay Foundation, please contact:

Hay House, Inc., P.O. Box 5100, Carlsbad, CA 92018-5100
(760) 431-7695 or (800) 654-5126
(760) 431-6948 (fax) or (800) 650-5115 (fax)
www.hayhouse.com® • www.hayfoundation.org

Published and distributed in Australia by: Hay House Australia Pty. Ltd., 18/36 Ralph St., Alexandria NSW 2015 • *Phone:* 612-9669-4299 *Fax:* 612-9669-4144 • www.hayhouse.com.au

Published and distributed in the United Kingdom by: Hay House UK, Ltd., Astley House, 33 Notting Hill Gate, London W11 3JQ • *Phone:* 44-20-3675-2450 • *Fax:* 44-20-3675-2451 • www.hayhouse.co.uk

Published and distributed in the Republic of South Africa by: Hay House SA (Pty), Ltd., P.O. Box 990, Witkoppen 2068 • *Phone/Fax:* 27-11-467-8904 • www.hayhouse.co.za

Published in India by: Hay House Publishers India, Muskaan Complex, Plot No. 3, B-2, Vasant Kunj, New Delhi 110 070 • *Phone:* 91-11-4176-1620 • *Fax:* 91-11-4176-1630 • www.hayhouse.co.in

Distributed in Canada by: Raincoast Books, 2440 Viking Way, Richmond, B.C. V6V 1N2 • *Phone:* 1-800-663-5714 • *Fax:* 1-800-565-3770 • www.raincoast.com

Take Your Soul on a Vacation

Visit www.HealYourLife.com® to regroup, recharge, and reconnect with your own magnificence.Featuring blogs, mind-body-spirit news, and life-changing wisdom from Louise Hay and friends.

Visit www.HealYourLife.com today!